Phonology and Reading Disability

PHONOLOGY AND READING DISABILITY
Solving the Reading Puzzle

Edited by
Donald Shankweiler, Ph.D.
Fellow, International Academy for Research
 in Learning Disabilities
Research Associate, Haskins Laboratories
Professor, University of Connecticut

and

Isabelle Y. Liberman, Ph.D.
Fellow, International Academy for Research
 in Learning Disabilities
Research Associate, Haskins Laboratories
Professor Emerita, University of Connecticut

**International Academy for Research in Learning
Disabilities Monograph Series, Number 6**

Ann Arbor   The University of Michigan Press

Copyright © by The University of Michigan 1989
All rights reserved
Published in the United States of America by
The University of Michigan Press
Manufactured in the United States of America

1992 1991 1990 1989   4 3 2 1

Library of Congress Cataloging-in-Publication Data

Phonology and reading disability : solving the reading puzzle / edited by Donald Shankweiler and Isabelle Y. Liberman.
    p.   cm.—(International Academy for Research in Learning Disabilities monograph series ; no. 6)
  Bibliography: p.
  ISBN 0-472-10133-1 (alk. paper)
  1. Reading disability—Congresses. 2. English language—Phonology—Congresses. 3. Reading—Remedial teaching—Congresses. I. Shankweiler, Donald. 1934– . II. Liberman, Isabelle Y., 1918–
III. Series.
LB1050.5.P49   1989
428.4′2—dc20   89-5163
                                                               CIP

*This series of monographs published under the
sponsorship of the International Academy for
Research in Learning Disabilities is dedicated
to the recognition of Professor Alexander
Romanovich Luria, Ph.D., of the Union of Soviet
Socialist Republics, a world-class professional
whose work underscores a major development in
an understanding of the neurophysiological development of learning disabled children and adults.*

International Academy for Research in Learning Disabilities
Members of the Research Monograph Publications Committee

Lynette L. Bradley, Ph.D.	*United Kingdom*
Luis Bravo-Valdivieso, Ph.D.	*Chile*
James H. Bryan, Ph.D.	*United States of America*
Uta Frith, Ph.D.	*United Kingdom*
Neil S. Gordon, M.D.	*United Kingdom*
Sasson S. Gubbay, M.D.	*Australia*
Merrill Hiscock, Ph.D.	*Canada*
E. Roy John, Ph.D.	*United States of America*
Ian A. McKinlay, F.R.C.P.	*United Kingdom*
Hanuš Papoušek, M.D., D.Sci.	*Federal Republic of Germany*
Diane Paul-Brown, Ph.D.	*Australia*
Cóstas D. Pórpodas, Ph.D.	*Greece*
Ronald E. Reeve, Ph.D.	*United States of America*
Otfried Spreen, Ph.D.	*Canada*
Mervyn Skuy, Ph.D.	*Republic of South Africa*
Christina E. van Kraayenoord, Ph.D.	*Australia*
Wlliam M. Cruickshank, Ph.D. Chairman	*United States of America*

The manuscript has been read by a minimum of three members of the Monograph Committee or by individuals not members of the Academy, but recognized as specialists in the area of the research. This study is recognized as significant by representatives of the Academy, but its publication by the Academy does not include International Academy for Research in Learning Disabilities endorsement of the research proposition, the methodology employed, or the conclusions reached. These are the sole responsibility of the authors. It is a pleasure for the Academy to make this research available to the academic community in the spirit of further securing solutions to the complexities of learning disabilities.

Preface

This monograph originated from an invitation to prepare a symposium on reading and language processes for a meeting of the International Academy for Research on Learning Disabilities that was held at Northwestern University, Evanston, Illinois, in October 1986. The symposium generated all the papers that follow except that of William E. Tunmer, which was added to permit a more comprehensive review. A lively discussion ensued at the symposium, following which IARLD Director William M. Cruickshank asked us to prepare this volume to permit wider circulation of these research findings and views.

Why should papers on reading be included in the monograph series of the Academy? We believe the papers to be appropriate because the problems of a large proportion of the children who are referred for special attention as learning disabled can be traced directly or indirectly to their difficulties in learning to read. Therefore, even for the clinicians, teachers, and researchers who are more broadly concerned with learning disabilities, a better understanding of the reading process and its particular difficulties can be a critical need. Our aim in this monograph is to begin to meet that need. To that end, we have examined some basic questions that we believe must be addressed if we are to succeed in overcoming reading failure and increasing literacy. We have considered such questions as why mastery of the alphabetic principle eludes so many children and is more difficult to attain than mastery of speaking and listening; the role of phonological processes in reading and the consequences of weaknesses in phonological capabilities; what the successful deaf reader can tell us about the reading process; how reading and listening comprehension are affected by phonetic coding in working memory; why some language structures are difficult to understand; how longitudinal studies can help to identify the causes of reading problems. Wherever possible, the implications of the findings for instruction and remediation are outlined.

Because this book reflects its origins in a half-day symposium, it necessarily omits discussion of many matters of concern to researchers. For instance, few details of experiments will be found here. The interested reader can consult the references at the end of each chapter to find these details and further interpretive discussion. A book like this one must also be selective in its coverage of research topics. Space did not permit the inclusion of some approaches that the authors and editors deem important. Promising recent information on the genetic study of reading disability is one example. Fortunately, reviews of this research may be found elsewhere.

Instead of a comprehensive overview of the whole field of reading disability research, then, these five chapters give a coherent account of what we take to be of primary importance: how reading is related to spoken language. Occasional differences in emphasis and interpretation will be found among the contributors, but it will also be apparent that they share a common point of view, although no attempt was made to force a consensus. The fact that the authors bring different research approaches and backgrounds to their work on reading is a strength, in our view, and makes the consensus the more believable.

Acknowledgments

Preparation of this volume was supported in part by a program project grant (HD-01994) to Haskins Laboratories from the National Institute of Child Health and Human Development. We are happy to record our gratitude to the Institute that has supported many of the investigations reported in this volume, and over the years, has contributed much to our research effort.

We had help from a number of people in preparing this volume. Foremost among them is Mrs. Alice Dadourian who has provided us with most expert and gracious assistance in all phases of the preparation of the manuscript. We are indebted to the following people for translations of the abstracts into French, German, and Spanish: Arthur S. Abramson, Paola Bellabarba, Terri Erwin, Jochen Machetanz, Daniel Recasens, Bruno Repp, and Ana Varela.

Contents

1. The Alphabetic Principle and Learning to Read   1
   Isabelle Y. Liberman, Donald Shankweiler,
   and Alvin M. Liberman

2. How Problems of Comprehension Are Related
   to Difficulties in Decoding   35
   Donald Shankweiler

3. Phonology and Reading: Evidence from
   Profoundly Deaf Readers   69
   Vicki L. Hanson

4. The Role of Language-Related Factors
   in Reading Disability   91
   William E. Tunmer

5. Why Poor Readers Misunderstand Spoken Sentences   133
   Stephen Crain

   Contributors   167

CHAPTER 1

The Alphabetic Principle and Learning to Read

Isabelle Y. Liberman, Donald Shankweiler, and Alvin M. Liberman

Abstract

Proper application of the alphabetic principle rests on an awareness of the internal phonological (and morphophonological) structure of words that the alphabet represents. Unfortunately for the would-be reader-writer, such awareness is not an automatic consequence of speaking a language, because the biological specialization for speech manages the production and perception of these structures below the level of consciousness. Not surprisingly, then, awareness of phonological structures is normally lacking in preliterate children and adults; the degree to which it does exist is the best single predictor of success in learning to read; lack of awareness usually yields to appropriate instruction; and such instruction makes for better readers. That some children have particular difficulty in developing phonological awareness (and in learning to read) is apparently to be attributed to a general deficiency in the phonological component of their natural capacity for language. Thus, these children are also relatively poor in short-term memory for verbal information, in perceiving speech in noise, in producing complex speech patterns, and in finding the words that name objects. All children will benefit from instruction that is intelligently designed to show them what the alphabet is about.

Résumé

L'application juste du principe alphabétique repose sur une intuition de la structure phonologique (et morphophonologique) interne des mots que représente l'alphabet. Quant au prétendu lecteur-écrivain, malheureusement, telle intuition n'est pas une conséquence automatique de parler une langue, parce que la spécialisation biologique pour la parole dirige la production et la perception de ces structures au-dessous du niveau de la conscience. Alors, on n'en est pas surpris que l'intuition des structures phonologiques manque normalement aux illetrés, et les enfants et les adultes. Le point jusqu'auqel elle existe, ça prédit le mieux que l'on réussira à apprendre à lire; le manque de cette intuition cède d'ordinaire à l'enseignement approprié; tel enseignement forme de meilleurs lecteurs. A cause, semble-t-il, d'un défaut général du composant phonologique de leur capacité naturelle de la langue, quelques enfants subissent des difficultés en développant l'intuition phonologique (et en apprenant à lire). Ainsi, ces enfants-là manquent quelque peu de mémoire de courte durée pour les renseignements verbaux, aussi bien que la faculté de percevoir la parole dans le bruit, d'énoncer des expressions complexes, et de trouver des mots qui nomment les objets. Tous les enfants profiteront de l'enseignement formé avec intelligence pour leur montrer de quoi s'agit l'alphabet.

Zusammenfassung

Die richtige Anwendung des alphabetischen Prinzips auf Sprache setzt voraus, daß die interne phonologische (und morphophonologische) Struktur der Wörter bekannt ist. Unglücklicherweise für den Schreiben/Lesenlernenden ergibt sich die Kenntnis dieser Struktur nicht automatisch aus der Fähigkeit, die Sprache zu sprechen, da die biologische Spezialisierung für Sprache Perception und Produktion dieser Strukturen ohne Einschaltung des Bewußtseins erlaubt. Es ist daher nicht überraschend, daß

Kindern und Erwachsenen vor dem Lesenlernen üblicherweise phonologische Strukturen nicht bewußt sind. Das Ausmaß, wieweit solche Strukturen bewußt sind, ist im Verlauf des Lesenlernens der beste Parameter für die Beurteilung des Lernerfolges. Meist ist es durch einfache Instruktionen möglich, diese Strukturen zu vermitteln, und die Lesefähigkeit kann verbessert werden. Die Tatsache, daß einige Kinder besondere Schwierigkeiten haben, phonologische Strukturen zu erfassen (und demzufolge Lesen zu lernen), muß offenbar einem allgemeinen Defekt in der phonologischen Komponente ihrer natürlichen Sprachkompetenz zugeschrieben werden. So haben diese Kinder ebenfalls Schwächen im Kurzzeitgedächtnis für verbale Informationen, in der Sprachperzeption unter Störeinflüssen, in der Produktion komplexer Sprachmuster und im Benennen von Gegenständen. Von ausnahmslos positivem Effekt für die betroffenen Kinder ist eine Lehrmethode, die in intelligenter Weise die Funktion des Alphabets vermittelt.

Resumen

Una aplicación adecuada del principio alfabético se basa en el conocimiento de la estructura fonológica (y morfofonológica) de las palabras que representa el alfabeto. Desafortunadamente para el lector-escritor potencial, tal conocimiento no es consecuencia automática de la capacidad del habla de una lengua, puesto que la especialización biológica para el habla comporta la producción y percepción de estas estructuras de modo inconsciente. Así pues, no es sorprendente que el conocimiento de las estructuras fonológicas esté ausente normalmente en los niños y en los adultos que todavía no han aprendido a leer ni a escribir; el grado de tal conocimiento es la mejor garantía de éxito en el aprendizaje de la lectura; la ausencia de conocimiento comporta normalmente una instrucción apropiada; y esta instrucción forma mejores lectores. El hecho de que algunos niños muestren una dificultad especial en el desarrollo del conocimiento fonológico (y en el aprendizaje de la lectura) se debe aparentemente a una deficiencia general en el componente fonológico de su capacidad natural para el lenguaje. Se da el caso de que estos niños también presentan una actuación bastante deficiente por lo que respecta a la memoria a corto plazo sobre información verbal, a la percepción del habla enmascarada con ruido, a la producción de estructuras complejas del habla, y a la búsqueda de palabras para nombrar objetos. Todos los niños deben beneficiarse de un tipo de instrucción que haya sido planificada inteligentemente para mostrarles en qué consiste el alfabeto.

For some fifteen years, we have been exploring the sources of the problems beginners encounter in learning to read. Since children are quite fluent in their native language when first encountering the language in print, we began by asking what seemed to us the obvious question: what is required of the child in reading a language but not in speaking or listening to it? The first answer that came to mind, of course, was the discrimination of the visual shapes of the letters. But investigators who had done comprehensive studies of many different aspects of the reading process (see Doehring 1968), or who had compiled exhaustive reviews of the visual factors involved in reading (Benton and Pearl 1978; Stanovich 1982; Vellutino 1979; Vernon 1957), were all in agreement that beginners who were making little progress in learning to read generally showed no significant difficulty in the visual identification of letters.

Beyond letter identification, reading requires mastery of a system that maps letter shapes to units of speech. However, as we noted years ago (Liberman 1973), there is no evidence that children of normal intelligence, given proper instruction, have difficulty in associating individual letters of the alphabet with their appropriate speech equivalents. Perhaps, then, they are defeated by the often complex and irregular relations in English between spelling and language. Surely, the complexities of English spelling do create some problems. But even when the items to be read include only those words that map the sound in a simple, consistent way, many children still fail (Savin 1972).

Learning to identify the letters, learning to associate them with consonant and vowel sounds, learning to cope with the irregularities of English spelling—none of these is the primary obstacle in learning to read. What is it then that makes reading so hard while speech is relatively so easy? In the seventies, we (Liberman 1971; Shankweiler and Liberman 1972) and other investigators (Elkonin 1973; Gleitman and Rozin 1977; Klima 1972; Mattingly 1972) proposed another possible source of difficulty in reading that is not present in speech. Although both reading and speech require some degree of mastery of language, reading requires, in addition, a mastery of the alphabetic principle. This entails an awareness of the internal phonological structure of the words of the language, an awareness that must be more explicit than is ever demanded in the ordinary course of listening and responding to speech. If this is so, it should follow that beginning learners with a weakness in phonological awareness would be at risk.

We here first set forth the considerations that led us to that view, followed by the evidence that supports it. Then we say why we should consider that deficits in awareness of the phonological structure may be only one symptom of a more general underlying deficiency in the phonological component of the beginning reader's capacity for language. Finally we consider the implications for instruction.

Phonology and the Alphabetic Principle

We begin, then, with the assumption that reading by an alphabetic writing system requires mastery of the alphabetic principle. Surprisingly, this assumption, which seems to us a truism, is not accepted by everyone in the field, as we will see. But even among those who think the principle important, many take it— we would say mistake it—to mean simply an understanding by the would-be reader that the discrete letters of the alphabet represent the discrete sounds of speech. Our view (Liberman 1983) is different. As we see it, the letters of the alphabet do not represent sounds as such, but rather the more remote phonological (and morphophonological) segments those sounds convey. This is not to quibble. For surely it must be somewhat confusing to children to be told that the word *bag* is spelled with three letters, when their ears tell them plainly that it has but one sound. The confusion is only worse confounded if the teacher insists, against the evidence of what the child hears, that *bag* can be divided into three sounds, and that these can then be "blended" so as to re-form the word. For there is, in fact, no way, with or without the marvels of modern technology, to divide *bag* into pieces of sound that correspond in any reasonable way to the sounds of the three letters, nor is there any way to synthesize the word by somehow putting the letter sounds together. Though bag does truly consist of three segments—it differs from *sag* in the first, from *big* in the second, and from *bat* in the third—these segments are to be found only in the underlying phonology, not in the surface appearances of the sound (Liberman et al. 1967).

To emphasize that letters stand for sounds also risks making it that much harder for a reader to understand perfectly reasonable aspects of English spelling—for example, *cats* and *dogs,* instead of *cats* and *dogz;* or *bat* and *batter,* instead of *bat* and *badder;* or *an apple,* instead of *uh napple;* and so on. As for those aspects of English spelling that are most egregiously unreasonable—for example, *through, rough,* and the like—we confess that even a proper understanding of the alphabetic principle is not likely to be of much help, but then neither will anything else, short of learning about how the language has changed since the orthography was developed. (Such spellings need not be a hindrance if they are introduced only after the more systematic aspects of the orthography have been understood.)

The identification of letters with sounds promotes yet another misunderstanding, this one about the nature of words and how they are perceived. For it accords all too well with the commonplace notion that it is only spoken words that are made of phonological units. Words that come to us via print are incorrectly thought to be different, in that they supposedly can (and perhaps should) be perceived independently of phonology. On this basis, some advise that the reader be taught from the very beginning to skip the phonology (read this as skipping the sound) and go "direct to meaning" (Goodman 1976; Smith 1971). Others grant that going through the phonology—which is taken to mean "sounding it out"—may be useful for the beginning reader, or for the mature reader who encounters a strange word, but they otherwise hold that the putatively "direct" (nonphonological) route is the way to go (Coltheart 1978; Waters, Seidenberg and Bruck 1984).

We believe that these assumptions seriously misconstrue the nature of words and the processes by which they are produced and perceived, in print as in speech. Consider, in this connection, a critical difference between language and all other natural forms of communication. In all the nonlinguistic systems—whether the medium is acoustic, optical, electrical, or chemical—meanings are conveyed by signals that differ holistically, one from another. That is to say that there are no words. The inevitable consequence is that the number of meanings that can be communicated is limited to the number of holistically different signals the animal can produce and perceive, a number that is always quite small. Even if that number can somehow be increased, there is no way of doing it so as to guarantee that the new signals will be immediately recognized as belonging naturally to a system that has a specifically communicative function.

Language is different in a most important way. Meanings are not conveyed directly by signals that differ holistically, but rather by words that are distinct from each other in their internal structure. This structure is formed of a small number of meaningless phonological segments we know as consonants and vowels, and governed according to a highly systematic combinatorial scheme called phonology. The consequence is that words can (and do) number in the tens of thousands. Moreover, there is a perfectly natural basis for accommodating new words, since the phonological system, which all speakers of the language have in common, automatically recognizes a new, but legal, structure as a word that stands ready to have meaning attached to it. It is only because children have this phonological system that they are able to acquire new words and their meanings with such astonishing ease and rapidity (Studdert-Kennedy 1987).

What follows, then, is that phonology governs all words, whether dead, living, or waiting to be born. So, whatever else a word is, and regardless of whether it is spoken or printed, it is always a phonological structure. If listeners or readers correctly perceive a word, they correctly perceive the structure that distinguishes it. They may very well be unsure of its meaning—indeed, may even have got the meaning wrong—but if they have the phonological structure, they have a perfectly adequate basis for ultimately getting its meaning properly sorted out. As for going directly to meaning—that is, independently of phonology—surely that is done when a person sees a picture, for example, or hears the roar of a lion, but not when one perceives a word as it is spoken or read.

From our point of view, then, there is no reason to ask, as some do, whether readers must, or should get to meaning via the phonology. To make sense of this question, one must make three false assumptions. The first is that the meanings can be communicated in language independently of words (that is, phonological structures), but in fact they cannot. The second is that the phonological units that form all words are equivalent to the sounds of speech, but in fact they are not. And the third is that an alphabetic transcription specifies, on a segment by segment basis, how the speech organs are to be articulated and coarticulated so as to produce the sounds of speech, but in fact it does not. What the reader must do is to match the alphabetic transcription to the abstract phonological structure of the word it represents. In the case of a familiar word, this structure and its associated meaning(s) are available in the reader's lexicon; in the case of an unfamiliar word, given a command of the alphabetic principle, the structure is easily formed and thus made ready for whatever meanings may subsequently be attached to it. Once the reader has the phonological form of the word, the appropriate phonetic structure and its associated articulatory movements are automatically available for use in working memory, or for reading aloud if the occasion should call for that.

Phonological Processing in Reading-Writing and in Listening-Speaking

Why is it normally so much harder and less natural to deal with phonological structures in reading and writing than it is in listening and speaking? A serious attempt to answer this question would take us quite deeply into the phonological system and its biology, for the answer requires explaining, among other things, why speech could have evolved in the history of our species but writing systems could not, and why speech can develop in the child without explicit instruction but reading and writing typically cannot (Liberman, in press). Here, we can offer only a truncated account.

Like all members of the animal kingdom, human beings have highly specialized ways of communicating with their fellows. In the human case, and only there, this specialization includes, as a critical component, the phonological system that, as we have seen, makes large vocabularies possible. As this system evolved in the race, and as it develops anew in each child, it employs abstract motor structures—let us call them gestures—that ultimately control the movements of the speech organs (Browman and Goldstein 1985; Liberman and Mattingly 1985; Liberman and Mattingly 1989). These gestures are adapted for one purpose and for one purpose only: the production of strings of consonants and vowels at rates many times more rapid than could otherwise be achieved. These rates, which run about eight to ten per second on average, are managed by precisely overlapping and merging the articulatory movements that produce the phonologically significant aspects of the speech sounds. This coarticulation, as it is called, is a most complex process, but it does not appear so in the normal exercise of speech functions, because it is done automatically and naturally by this aspect of the specialization for language. A consequence is that a neurologically normal child, put in a speech environment, can hardly be prevented from learning to form phonological structures and to exploit coarticulation for that purpose. (Lacking this specialization, nonhuman primates do not, and cannot, learn to produce these structures; this is to say that they cannot produce words.) A more important consequence for our purposes is that to speak a word one need not know how it is spelled. The speaker need only think of the word; the phonological component of his grammar "spells" it for him. Indeed, the automaticity of this specialization makes it that much harder to be aware of how the word is spelled, or even to know that such a thing as spelling exists.

Perception of the speech signal is correspondingly complex and automatic. Given coarticulation, there is no direct correspondence between the phonological structure intended by the speaker and the surface properties of the sound. Most relevant to our concerns is the fact that, as we have so often pointed out, the number of segments in the sound is not equal to the number of segments in the phonological structure it conveys (Liberman et al. 1967). Thus, the three consonants and vowels of a word like *bag* are so thoroughly coarticulated as to produce a single segment of sound. But this is no problem for listeners, for they have only to rely on their phonological specialization to automatically process the speech signal and recover the coarticulated gestures that caused it (Liberman and Mattingly 1989). It is a problem for would-be readers, however, because, given the complex relation between phonological structure and sound, and the automaticity with which this relation is dealt in speech, they find it just that much harder to be aware that the word does have an internal structure and thus to appreciate why an alphabetic transcription makes sense.

Small wonder then that an alphabetic writing system is such a comparatively recent development in the history of our species. In contrast to the naturally evolved phonological structures it represents, it is an artifact. The development of this artifact had to wait on the discovery—and it was a discovery—that words have an internal structure. Once that discovery was available, someone could and did invent the notion that, by representing the units of that structure with arbitrarily chosen optical shapes, people could read and write all the words of the language—those they were already familiar with and those they had yet to encounter. But they could exploit this wonderful invention only if they understood the discovery on which it was based.

Awareness of Phonological Structure and Reading

Development of Phonological Awareness in Children

Considerations such as these led us at the very outset of our research on reading to suppose that preliterate children would not naturally have made the discovery that underlay the invention of the alphabet, from which it would follow that they would not be prepared to understand and apply the alphabetic principle. So we began to examine developmental trends in phonological awareness by testing the ability of young children to segment words into their constituent elements. We investigated the children's segmentation of spoken words both by syllable and phoneme (Liberman et al. 1974). (The latter class of units of the phonological representation comprise the consonants and vowels. Heretofore we have referred to these only by the general term *phonological segments*. From now on we will call then *phonemes* to distinguish them from syllables.) We found that normal preschool children performed rather poorly, but that the phonemes presented the greater difficulty by far.

It was clear from these results that awareness of phoneme segments, the basic units of the alphabetic orthography, is initially harder to achieve than awareness of syllable segments, and develops later, if at all. More relevant to our present purposes, it was also apparent that a large number of children, about 30 percent of our sample, had not attained an understanding of the internal phonemic structure of words, even at the end of a full year in school. Surely, they are the ones we need to worry about, because they are the ones who are deficient in the linguistic awareness that may provide entry into the alphabetic system.

Lack of Phonological Awareness and Reading
Failure in Children

Is lack of phonological awareness in fact related to failure in reading and writing? That the answer is yes is strongly supported by studies in a number of languages. In English, the relation has been found, for example, in studies by Blachman (1984), Bradley and Bryant (1983), Fox and Routh (1980), Goldstein (1976), Helfgott (1976), Treiman and Baron (1981) and Vellutino and Scanlon (1987). Their findings have been supported by studies in Swedish by Lundberg and associates (Lundberg, Olofsson and Wall 1980) and Magnusson and Naucler (1987), in Spanish by de Manrique and Gramigna (1984), in French by a group of Belgian researchers (Alegria, Pignot, and Morais 1982), and recently in Italian by Cossu and associates (Cossu et al. 1988).

The study carried out by Lundberg and his associates in Sweden (Lundberg, Olofsson, and Wall 1980) is worthy of special mention on two counts. It provides one of the most intensive examinations of the linguistic abilities of kindergartners. It is noteworthy as well because it also addresses the question of whether the children's deficiency is, in fact, linguistic or whether it might be attributable to a deficiency in general analytic ability. Their battery of eleven tests given to 200 kindergartners included both linguistic and nonlinguistic tasks. In the linguistic set were: (1) word synthesis tasks that varied in two dimensions of two levels each—with or without memory load and using either phoneme or syllable units, and (2) word analysis tasks analogous to those for synthesis and, in addition, three others demanding analysis of phoneme position in words, reversal of phoneme segments in words, and rhyming. Since the linguistic tasks required the child to shift attention from meaning to abstract form, thus possibly reflecting a general cognitive function not exclusively limited to linguistic material, nonlinguistic control tasks that simulated those cognitive demands were also included. The most powerful predictors of later reading and writing skills in the entire battery turned out to be those requiring phonological awareness, specifically the analytic ability to manipulate phonemes in words. In contrast, the poor readers showed no particular deficiency in the nonlinguistic tasks.

These findings that tasks of linguistic, rather than nonlinguistic analysis, and specifically phonemic analysis, were predictive of reading failure have since received support from other studies here and abroad. For example, in a study of six to nine year olds with severe reading disability (Morais, Cluytens, and Alegria 1984) it was found that these children were poorer on segmenting words into their constituent parts but performed just as well as normal readers in a matched task that required them to deal analytically with musical tone sequences instead of words. The question of a possible general analytic deficit was also addressed in two complementary experiments, one with good and poor readers in the third grade and the other with good and poor readers in adult education classes (Pratt 1985). All the subjects were given three linguistic awareness tests and one nonspeech control task identical in format to one of the linguistic measures. Significant differences were found between the good and poor readers at both age levels on all three linguistic measures, but not on the nonspeech control task. Thus the poor readers, whether young or old, had no more difficulty in segmental analysis than the good readers when the task was nonlinguistic; their problem was limited to the segmental analysis of speech.

Not only reading, but early spelling proficiency has also been found to be closely related to analytic phonological skills. In a study of kindergartners (Liberman et al. 1985), the children's ability to produce invented spellings, given only some knowledge of letter names (see Read 1986), was related to their performance on a series of language-based tasks. It was found that the children's proficiency in spelling was more closely tied to phonological awareness than to any of the other aspects of language development tested. Of the eight tasks in the study, only the three that unquestionably tapped phonological analysis skills made a difference statistically. They combined to account for 93 percent of the variance in proficiency in invented spelling. A phoneme analysis test patterned after Lundberg, Olofsson, and Wall (1980) made the largest contribution—67 percent of the variance. A test of the ability to write letters to phoneme dictation accounted for 20 percent more, and a phoneme deletion task ("Say *milk* without the *m*") added another 6 percent. (A fourth task, picture naming, added 1 percent, but did not reach significance in the correlation. As we will note later, however, naming can be a subtle indicator of more general phonological difficulties.)

Among the four language-based tests that did not contribute to the invented spelling performance were three that are frequently included in clinical evaluations: receptive vocabulary, articulation as measured by the repetition of simple words, and letter naming or writing. The fourth was a syllable deletion test ("Say *bookcase* without the *book*"). Being able to segment words by syllable was, as we would expect, not enough to equip the child to produce alphabetically written words.

The Remedial Effect of Training in Awareness

Given the abundant evidence that phonological awareness is predictive of success in reading, it is of interest to know that such awareness can be trained even in preschool and kindergarten (Bradley and Bryant 1983; Content et al. 1982; Lundberg, Frost, and Petersen 1988; Olofsson and Lundberg 1983). It is of special interest to find, moreover, that the training can have a salutary effect on future reading skill. Impressive evidence for the efficacy of the training comes from a pair of experiments by

Bradley and Bryant (1983). The first experiment confirmed the high correlations found by others between preschoolers' phonological awareness and later reading skill. This was done by a comparison of children's performance on rhyming tasks and their achievement in reading and spelling several years later. The second experiment was directed to an examination of the effect of various kinds of early training on the later academic achievements of children considered to be at risk for failure. To this end, the children who had been found in the first experiment to have a low level of phonological awareness were divided into four groups. One group was trained to sort pictured words on cards by phonological categories. A second received the same training except that letters corresponding to the phonemic categories were added. A third group was trained to sort by semantic categories. A control group was given equal time and unrelated card play. The two phonologically trained groups were found to be superior to the others in subsequent tests of reading and spelling. Moreover, in follow-up studies, they continued to maintain their advantage.

Further evidence for the positive effect of early training in phonological awareness is found in the longitudinal study by Lundberg and associates (Lundberg, Frost, and Petersen 1988). An experimental group of kindergartners who had participated in a variety of analytic word games was found at year-end to be superior in phoneme awareness to a matched control group. When compared in academic achievement in the first grade, the experimental group was slightly below the controls in math and IQ but significantly superior in both reading and spelling. Moreover their advantage was maintained when the children were retested in the second grade.

Lack of Phonological Awareness
and Adult Literacy

What about phonological awareness in adult nonreaders? Is it still a problem for them? The question as to whether phonological awareness improves spontaneously with age or requires some form of instruction is a crucial one, with obvious implications not only for preschool instruction but also for the design of literacy teaching programs geared to adolescents and adults. This question was explored in an unusual investigation by a Belgian research group who examined the phonological awareness of illiterate adults in a rural area of Portugal (Morais et al. 1979). They found that the illiterate adults could neither delete nor add phonemes at the beginning of nonsense words, whereas others from the same community who had received reading instruction in an adult literacy class succeeded in performing those tasks. The authors concluded that awareness of phoneme segmentation does not develop spontaneously even by adulthood but arises as a concomitant of reading instruction and experience.

In view of these findings, we believed it would prove of value to test the phonological awareness of adults who had had reading instruction but were nonetheless poor readers. To this end, our reading research group (Liberman et al. 1985) tested the members of a community literacy class, all of whom were having serious decoding problems despite years of schooling. What we found was that these adults performed with difficulty on a very simple task in which the subjects were required only to identify the initial, medial, or final sound in monosyllabic words. Though this is an exercise that one might expect a first grader to be able to perform, our adults managed to produce correct responses on only 58 percent of the items. Moreover, they clearly found it to be singularly frustrating and unpleasant. This inability of adults with literacy problems to perform well on tasks demanding explicit understanding of phonological structure has also been found by other investigators—Byrne and Ledez (1983) in Australia, Marcel (1980) in England, and Read and Ruyter (1985) in a prison population in the United States.

A Broader Phonological Deficiency and Reading

Why do some people have difficulty in achieving the understanding of phonological structure that application of the alphabetic principle requires? One possibility, as we noted before, is that they may suffer from a general deficiency in the ability to divide objects of all kinds into their constituent elements. But as we pointed out, the results of several studies suggest that the difficulty is specifically linguistic. Another possibility—one that we and others have pursued—is that the poor reader's difficulty with analyzing words into their constituent units is one among several symptoms of a general deficiency in the phonological component of the child's natural capacity for language. If the underlying biology tends to set up phonological structures weakly, then it should follow that these structures would be that much harder for the child to bring to a level of explicit awareness. But there would be other consequences for the processing of language, and these we consider below.

Problems in Short-Term Memory
and Sentence Comprehension

Because short-term memory depends on the ability to gain access to phonological structure and to use it to hold linguistic information (Conrad 1964; Liberman, Mattingly, and Turvey 1972), we might expect people who have underlying phonological deficiencies to show various limitations on verbal tasks that tap short-term memory. This expectation is amply borne out.

The research literature contains many reports that young children who are poor readers are deficient in short-term memory. Typically they retain fewer items from a set of fixed size than age-matched good readers (see Mann, Liberman, and Shankweiler 1980; Shankweiler et al. 1985; Shankweiler, Smith, and Mann 1984; Wagner and Torgesen 1987). However, memory difficulties for poor readers appear to arise only under specific conditions; chiefly, they occur when the items to be retained are words and nameable objects. When the test materials do not lend themselves to verbal (i.e., phonological) encoding, as in memory for nonsense shapes or unfamiliar faces, memory testing does not find poor readers at a disadvantage (Katz, Shankweiler, and Liberman 1981; Liberman et al. 1982). The problem seems, therefore, to be a material-specific one, not an all-embracing memory impairment.

It is noteworthy, in addition, that memory differences between good and poor readers may also depend on other demands of the task—tasks that require rote recall of a list of unstructured items may be less differentiating than tasks that require both storage and further processing of the incoming material as in sentence processing (Daneman and Carpenter 1980; Perfetti and Goldman 1976). Since language structures are hierarchically organized and sequentially transmitted, comprehension of language, either by ear or by eye, depends on a short-term memory system that transiently stores and continuously processes the incoming segments of the linguistic message. In keeping with current usage (see Baddeley and Hitch 1974; also Shankweiler and Crain 1986), we call this form of memory *working memory,* a term which is used throughout this book. A phonological deficiency would understandably impair the functions of working memory and could be expected, in turn, to have repercussions on comprehension, whether of spoken discourse or printed text. For example, in sentence processing, the parsing of phonological segments into lexical units and the groupings of these units into higher-level phrasal structures requires phased control of the flow of linguistic information through the language apparatus.

We could therefore expect that children with reading disability would sometimes comprehend sentences poorly because of their difficulties in setting up and retaining phonological structures. The difficulty should be especially acute in reading, where the problem of decoding from print would create an additional processing load in an unskilled reader who decodes poorly. The important insight that the lower-level and higher-level reading problems of the poor reader are causally connected through constriction of working memory was contributed by Perfetti and Lesgold (1979). In their terms, poor decoding skills coupled with the limitations of working memory create in the poor reader a "bottleneck" in information flow with severe repercussions for comprehension.

But, as Crain and Shankweiler will discuss in later chapters of this volume, comprehension difficulties of poor readers are not limited to reading. From our working memory perspective, difficulties should also arise in spoken language processing, especially if the sentence material contains remote dependencies or structural ambiguities that necessitate reanalysis, or if the comprehension task presents additional complexities that further dilute memory resources. Several reports in the literature indicate that disabled readers do have problems in comprehending such sentences in spoken form as well as in reading (Byrne 1981; Mann, Shankweiler, and Smith 1984; Stein, Cairns, and Zurif 1984). More recent findings (which will be discussed in later chapters) indicate that the poor readers fail not because they lag behind their good reading peers in comprehension of grammar as such, but because working memory is overloaded due to deficient phonological processing.

By changing the task in various ways to reduce the demands on memory while testing the same grammatical structures, it has been shown that poor readers can succeed as well as good readers in comprehending complex grammatical structures (Crain et al., forthcoming; Smith et al., forthcoming). Thus, a memory impairment stemming from a weakness in phonological processing can masquerade as a grammatical or semantic deficit.

Other Language-Related Problems

Thus far we have discussed difficulties involving the phonological components of language that directly affect reading. Reading is affected both by the difficulties of accessing and mentally manipulating phonemic segments and by the limitations on use of the working memory that we have just discussed (though in the case of working memory the consequences are not confined to reading). We now turn to other deficits displayed by poor readers that are phonological in nature, but do not affect reading directly. These are worth mentioning, both for their diagnostic value, and because they add to the weight of the evidence that all the elements of the syndrome of many poor readers may stem ultimately from a deficiency in phonological processing.

One such deficit is suggested by some preliminary research into the speech perception of poor readers that was carried out by Brady and associates at Haskins Laboratories (Brady, Shankweiler, and Mann 1983). In their experiments, good and poor readers were tested on two auditory perception tasks, one involving words and the other nonspeech environmental sounds. The identification tasks were presented under two conditions—with favorable and unfavorable noise ratios. The findings were that the poor readers did show a deficit, but it was specific to the speech stimuli and occurred only in the noise-masked condition. They did not differ from the good readers in the perception of nonspeech environmental sounds, whether the sounds were noise-masked or not. Note that the poor readers apparently needed a higher quality of signal than the good readers for error-free performance in speech, but not for nonspeech environmental sounds. These results suggest that the minor deficit displayed by the poor readers may derive from phonological structures that are set up more weakly than in good readers, or are more difficult to activate.

Additional evidence for a broader phonological deficit in poor readers is provided by a study of speech production, specifically, the errors of junior high school students (Catts 1986). The critical finding was that the reading-disabled students made significantly more errors than matched normals on three different tasks in which their speech production was stressed. The author concluded, as we would, that their difficulties in speech production may be an extension of deficits in the phonological realm.

More evidence for a broad phonological deficit in poor readers was provided by a study of the performance of second graders on a naming test (Katz 1986). This study confirmed what others had shown—that poor readers named more words incorrectly. But it went further to show that their difficulties are often phonological and not semantic, as might be assumed. Three kinds of evidence were presented in this regard. First, when quizzed about the characteristics of the object they had named incorrectly (e.g., "tornado" for volcano), the poor readers were often able to describe it accurately. They clearly knew what the object was. That is, they described a volcano, not a tornado. Second, given the name of the item, they could select it from a group of pictured objects. That is, they could identify it correctly. And third, their naming errors were often related to the phonological and not the semantic aspect of the word. For example, though the name given to the picture of a volcano was incorrect, it shared syllable count, stress pattern, and vowels with the target word.

Distorted production of the word for an item that had been correctly identified could stem either from deficient specification of the phonological structure in the lexicon, or from deficient retrieval and processing of the stored phonological information. In either case, the source of the difficulty relates to the phonological structure of the words and not to their meanings.

Phonology and the Successful Deaf Reader

The congenitally deaf constitute a population with a phonological impairment arising from an entirely different source. Surprisingly, this group represents some of the most compelling evidence for the importance of phonological abilities for reading. It is well known that profound deafness from birth or early life usually results in attainment of a low level of reading skill. The hearing impaired of all ages tend to read far below grade expectations. But, nonetheless, differences in reading achievement are related to differences in phonological abilities even in deaf populations. Moreover, a few congenitally, profoundly deaf individuals can read well, even up to the college level.

How are these successful deaf readers different from the majority? Vicki Hanson and her associates at Haskins Laboratories asked that question in a series of experiments (Hanson 1982; Hanson and Fowler 1987; Hanson, Liberman, and Shankweiler 1984), which she will report on in detail in chapter 3. Briefly, they found that the successful deaf readers were not limited to reading English words as if they were logographs; that is, they were not, as one might assume, dependent on a limited store of words learned in paired associate fashion as visual designs. The results, which are discussed in detail in the chapter by Hanson, showed that unlike their poor reading peers among the deaf, these subjects, despite so little exposure to sound, were able to access phonological knowledge both in reading and in retaining verbal material in short-term memory.

In reading, the good readers among the deaf displayed their phonological sensitivity by responding differentially to rhyming and nonrhyming pairs of words (*save/wave* vs. *have/cave*) and by being able to name the real word equivalents of nonwords (*flame* for f-l-a-i-m; *tall* for t-a-u-l). In a short-term memory experiment, the successful deaf readers were more affected by phonetically confusing words than by those that were orthographically confusing or whose signs were formationally confusing. These results certainly suggest that successful deaf readers are using phonological processing, a conclusion also reached by Conrad with a less severely impaired population of deaf readers (Conrad 1979).

The question of how the congenitally, profoundly deaf might develop phonological sensitivity without being able to hear the sounds of speech is explored by Hanson (in this volume). She identifies several sources of information that may be helpful. The orthography itself tells them something about the systematic phonological forms of words. In addition, oral training when available supplies information about the gestures used to produce speech. Lipreading also provides considerable useable information, and the deaf individual's own attempts at speech may reflect more phonological sensitivity than is apparent to the hearing listener.

The Alphabetic Principle and Learning to Read

Implications for Instruction

In view of all the evidence that has accumulated in the past fifteen years to support the critical importance of phonological sensitivity for the attainment of literacy in an alphabetic system, one would surely expect teacher training to reflect these findings. Unfortunately, all too often it does not. Many teachers are being trained to teach reading without themselves ever having learned how an alphabetic orthography represents the language, why it is important for beginners to understand how the internal phonological structure of words relates to the orthography, or why it is hard for children to achieve this understanding.

In fact, teachers are all too often being provided with an instructional procedure that directs them specifically not to trouble the learner with details of how the alphabet works. Instead, they are told to view reading as a "guessing game" (Goodman 1976) in which the general import of the message, and not the actual words of the text, is to be emphasized. Beginners are encouraged to memorize the appearance of words as visual patterns by whatever means they can muster and to use their store of memorized words and their "whole language" capability as a basis for guessing the rest of the message from picture cues and context. Thus, they are not to be corrected when reading "kids" for *children* in a story about a playground, "Crest" for *toothpaste* in a story about dental hygiene, and "cats" for *dogs* in a story about pets.

Fortunately, many children—the lucky 75 percent or so who learn to read whatever the method—manage to pick up the alphabetic principle without much explicit instruction, if any. That is, given experience with printed material, they begin to discover for themselves the commonalities between similarly spoken and written words. When tested in kindergarten, these children turn out to be the ones with strengths in the phonological domain. For the large group of children with phonological deficiencies who do not understand that the spoken word has segments, and who have not discovered on their own that there is a correspondence between those segments and the segments of the printed word, the current vogue for the so-called (and from our point of view, misnamed) psycholinguistic guessing game and its offshoots, the "whole language" and "language experience" approaches, are likely to be disastrous. Many children taught this way are likely to join the ranks of the millions of functional illiterates in our country who stumble along, guessing at the printed message from their inadequate store of memorized words, unable to decipher a new word they have never seen before.

For those beginners who do not discover the alphabetic principle unaided, an introductory method that provides them with direct instruction in what they need to know is critical (Liberman 1985; Liberman and Shankweiler 1979). Direct instruction could begin with language analysis activities that are incorporated into the daily reading lesson. These activities can take many different forms, limited in number and variety only by the creativity of the teacher. The Auditory Discrimination in Depth Program of Lindamood and Lindamood (1975) is an ingenious method for helping the student to apprehend the internal phonological structure of words. It does this by calling the student's attention to the perceived distinctiveness of the articulatory gestures for the various phonemic constituents of spoken words and then demonstrating their sequences in syllables with variously colored blocks. The method was originally developed for individual reading remediation, but is currently being adapted for classroom use.

Adaptations of three exercises that we advocated some years ago (Liberman et al. 1980) have recently been shown by one of our colleagues (Blachman 1987) to be effective in improving reading skills even in an inner city school with a high incidence of reading failure. They are outlined in figure 1. In the first procedure, one originally devised by the Soviet educator Elkonin (1973), Blachman presents the child with a simple line drawing representing the word to be analyzed. A rectangle under the drawing is divided into squares equal in number to the phonemes

The Alphabetic Principle and Learning to Read

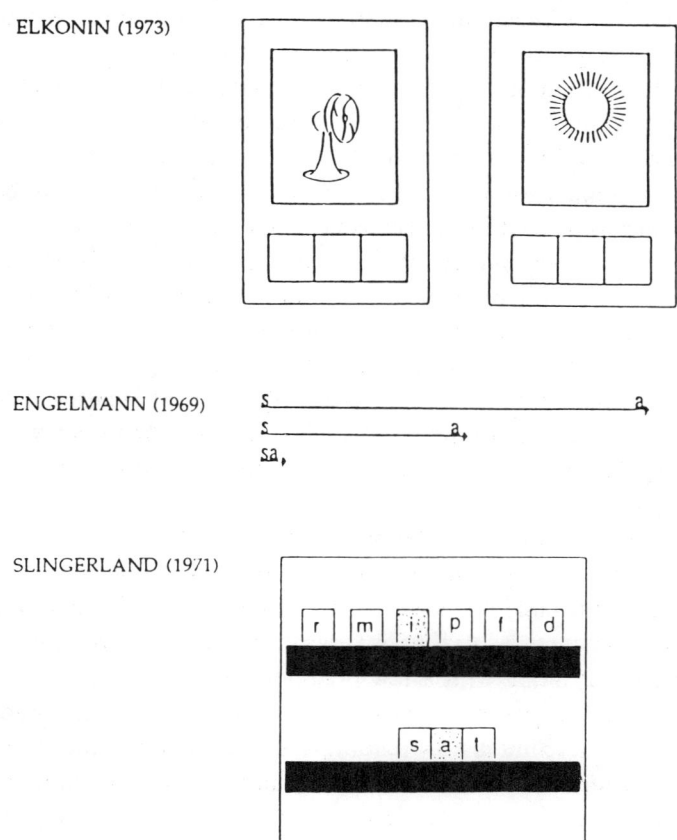

Fig. 1. Language analysis activities. (After Blachman 1987 and Liberman et al. 1980.)

in the picture word. The children are taught to say the word slowly, placing a counter in the appropriate squares of the diagram as the word is being slowly articulated. The words selected must begin with a fricative, liquid, or nasal rather than a stop consonant in order to permit their component phonemes to be accessed readily. Later, as the child progresses, the counters are color-coded—one color for vowels, another for consonants. Letter symbols can be added as well. In another activity, this one adapted from Engelmann (1969), the children are taught how to read as a single unit the combination of a consonant followed by a vowel. For example, the teacher writes a consonant on the blackboard (preferably, a fricative, nasal, or liquid)—the letter *s,* for example—and produces it, holding it over time until she writes the vowel and pronounces that. The length of time between the pronunciations of the initial consonant and the vowel (as well as a line drawn between them on the board) is then reduced step by step until the two phonemes are pronounced as a single unit— "sa". By adding stop consonants in the final position and pronouncing the resultant words, the children can begin to accumulate a pool of real words (sag, sat, sad, etc.). Thereafter, new vowels and new consonants can be introduced in the same way, and built into new words that are incorporated into stories to be read and written.

A similar effect can be produced by a third procedure, adapted from Slingerland (1971), in which a small pocket chart is used by the child at each desk to manipulate individual letters to form new words and learn new phonemes. The words thus constructed, along with a few nonphonetic "sight" words, can be used in stories and poems to be read and written by the child. Note that the child is now reading and writing words the structure of which is no longer a mystery and the understanding of which can be used productively to form related words (bag, bat, bad, big, bit, bid, etc.).

All these language analysis activities and others like them can be played as games in which the introduction of each new element not only informs but delights. Beginning readers with adequate phonological ability will require only a relatively brief exposure to such activities. They will soon develop skills that will enable them to decode the new words of the text and to go from them to the meaning of the passage. For such readers, language analysis can be quickly followed, or even accompanied, by practice with interesting reading materials from other sources. These children will benefit from the added skill that comes from increased reading practice and the further enhancement of vocabulary and knowledge that comes with expanded reading and life experience. But unless they receive extra assistance, the many beginners with weakness in phonological skills, who may include as many as 20 to 25 percent of the children, will remain locked into a sight-word stage of reading, able to cope only with those few words they have already memorized. They will not learn to decode new words—the essence of true reading skill—unless the method initially includes more intensive, direct, and systematic training in phonological structure and demonstrates how it relates to the way words are written. Research support for this view has been available for at least twenty years (see Chall 1967 or Pflaum et al. 1980). It is surely time to put the research into practice.

NOTE

Parts of this chapter were adapted from "Phonology and the problems of learning to read and write," *Remedial and Special Education*, 6 (1985):8–17. This research was supported in part by grant HD-01994 to Haskins Laboratories and by grant NIH-21888 to Yale University and Haskins Laboratories from the National Institute of Child Health and Human Development.

REFERENCES

Alegria, J.; Pignot, E.; and Morais, J. 1982. Phonetic analysis of speech and memory codes in beginning readers. *Memory and Cognition* 10:451–56.

Baddeley, A. D., and Hitch, G. 1974. Working memory. In *The Psychology of Learning and Motivation,* vol. 8, ed. G. H. Bower. New York: Academic Press.

Benton, A. L., and Pearl, D. 1978. *Dyslexia: An Appraisal of Current Knowledge.* New York: Oxford University Press.

Blachman, B. 1984. The relationships of rapid naming ability and language analysis skills to kindergarten and first grade reading achievement. *Journal of Educational Psychology* 76:610–22.

———. 1987. An alternative classroom reading program for learning disabled and other low-achieving children. In *Intimacy with Language: A Forgotten Basic in Teacher Education,* ed. W. Ellis. Baltimore: Orton Dyslexia Society.

Bradley, L., and Bryant, P. E. 1983. Categorizing sounds and learning to read—a causal connection. *Nature* 301:419–21.

Brady, S. A.; Shankweiler, D.; and Mann, V. A. 1983. Speech perception and memory coding in relation to reading ability. *Journal of Experimental Child Psychology* 35:345–67.

Browman, C. P., and Goldstein, L. M. 1985. Dynamic modeling of phonetic structure. In *Phonetic Linguistics,* ed. V. Fromkin. New York: Academic Press.

Byrne, B. 1981. Deficient syntactic control in poor readers: Is a weak phonetic memory code responsible? *Applied Psycholinguistics* 2: 201–12.

Byrne, B., and Ledez, J. 1983. Phonological awareness in reading-disabled adults. *Australian Journal of Psychology* 35:185–97.

Catts, H. W. 1986. Speech production/phonological deficits in reading disordered children. *Journal of Learning Disabilities* 19 (8): 504–8.

Chall, J. 1967. *Learning to Read: The Great Debate.* New York: McGraw Hill.

Coltheart, M. 1978. Lexical access in simple reading tasks. In *Strategies in Information Processing,* ed. G. Underwood. London: Academic Press.

Conrad, R. 1964. Acoustic confusions in immediate memory. *British Journal of Psychology* 55:75–84.

———. 1979. *The Deaf Child.* London: Harper and Row.

Content, A.; Morais, J.; Alegria, J.; and Bertelson, P. 1982. Accelerating the development of phonetic segmentation skills in kindergarteners. *Cahiers de psychologie cognitive* 2:259–69.

Cossu, G.; Shankweiler, D.; Liberman, I. Y.; Tola, G.; and Katz, L. 1988. Awareness of phonological segments and reading ability in Italian children. *Applied Psycholinguistics* 9:1–16.

Crain, S.; Shankweiler, D.; Macaruso, P.; and Bar-Shalom, E. Forthcoming. Working memory and sentence comprehension: Investigations of children with reading disorder. In *Neuropsychological Impairments of Short-Term Memory,* ed. G. Vallar and T. Shallice. Cambridge: Cambridge University Press.

Daneman, M., and Carpenter, P. A. 1980. Individual differences in working memory and reading. *Journal of Verbal Learning and Verbal Behavior* 19:450–66.

Doehring, D. G. 1968. *Patterns of Impairment in Specific Reading Disability.* Bloomington: Indiana University Press.

Elkonin, D. B. 1973. U.S.S.R. In *Comparative Reading,* ed. J. Downing. New York: Macmillan.

Englemann, S. 1969. *Preventing Failure in the Primary Grades.* Chicago: Science Research Associates.

Fox, B., and Routh, D. K. 1980. Phonetic analysis and severe reading disability in children. *Journal of Psycholinguistic Research* 9:115–19.

Gleitman, L. R., and Rozin, P. 1977. The structure and acquisition of reading. Relations between orthographies and structure of language. In *Toward a Psychology of Reading*, ed. A. S. Reber and D. L. Scarborough. Hillsdale, N.J.: Erlbaum.

Goldstein, D. M. 1976. Cognitive-linguistic functioning and learning to read in preschoolers. *Journal of Educational Psychology* 68: 680–88.

Goodman, K. S. 1976. Reading: A psycholinguistic guessing game. In *Theoretical Models and Processes of Reading*, ed. H. Singer and R. B. Ruddell. Newark, Del.: International Reading Association.

Hanson, V. L. 1982. Short-term recall by deaf signers of American Sign Language: Implications of encoding strategy for order recall. *Journal of Experimental Psychology: Learning, Memory, and Cognition* 8:572–83.

Hanson, V. L., and Fowler, C. A. 1987. Phonological coding in word reading: Evidence from hearing and deaf readers. *Memory and Cognition* 15 (3): 199–207.

Hanson, V. L.; Liberman, I. Y.; and Shankweiler, D. 1984. Linguistic coding by deaf children in relation to beginning reading success. *Journal of Experimental Child Psychology* 37:398–93.

Helfgott, J. 1976. Phoneme segmentation and blending skills of kindergarten children: Implications for beginning reading acquisition. *Contemporary Education Psychology* 1:157–69.

Katz, R. B. 1986. Phonological deficiencies in children with reading disability: Evidence from an object-naming task. *Cognition* 22: 225–57.

Katz, R. B.; Shankweiler, D.; and Liberman, I. Y. 1981. Memory for item order and phonetic recoding in the beginning reader. *Journal of Experimental Child Psychology* 32:474–84.

Klima, E. S. 1972. How alphabets might reflect language. In *Language by Ear and by Eye: The Relationships between Speech and Reading*, ed. J. F. Kavanagh and I .G Mattingly. Cambridge, Mass: MIT Press.

Liberman, A. M. in press. Reading is hard just because listening is easy. In *Wenner-Gren International Symposium Series: Brain and Reading*, ed. C. Von Euler. Hampshire, England: Macmillan.

Liberman, A. M.; Cooper, F. S.; Shankweiler, D. P.; and Studdert-Kennedy, M. 1967. Perception of the speech code. *Psychological Review* 74:431–61.

Liberman, A. M., and Mattingly, I. G. 1985. The motor theory of speech perception revised. *Cognition* 21:1–36.

———. 1989. A specialization for speech perception. *Science* 243: 489–94.

Liberman, I. Y. 1971. Basic research in speech and lateralization of language: Some implications for reading disability. *Bulletin of the Orton Society* 21:71–87.

———. 1973. Segmentation of the spoken word and reading acquisition. *Bulletin of the Orton Society* 23:65–77.

———. 1983. A language-oriented view of reading and its disabilities. In *Progress in Learning Disabilities*, Vol. 5, ed. H. Myklebust. New York: Grune and Stratton.

———. 1985. Should so-called modality preferences determine the nature of instruction for children with learning disabilities? In *Dyslexia: A neuroscientific approach to clinical evaluation*, ed. F. H. Duffy and N. Geschwind. Boston: Little, Brown.

Liberman, I. Y.; Mann, V.; Shankweiler, D.; and Werfelman, M. 1982. Children's memory for recurring linguistic and nonlinguistic material in relation to reading ability. *Cortex* 18:367–75.

Liberman, I. Y.; Rubin, H.; Duques, S.; and Carlisle, J. 1985. Linguistic abilities and spelling proficiency in kindergartners and adult poor spellers. In *Biobehavioral Measures of Dyslexia*, ed. J. Kavanagh and D. Gray. Parkton, Md.: York Press.

Liberman, I. Y., and Shankweiler, D. 1979. Speech, the alphabet and teaching to read. In *Theory and Practice of Early Reading*, ed. L. B. Resnik and P. A. Weaver. Hillsdale, N.J.: Erlbaum.

———. 1985. Phonology and the problems of learning to read and write. *Remedial and Special Education* 6:8–17.

Liberman, I. Y.; Shankweiler, D.; Blachman, B.; Camp, L; and Werfelman, M. 1980. Steps toward literacy. In *Auditory Processing and Language: Clinical and Research Perspectives*, ed. P. Levinson and C. Sloan. New York: Grune and Stratton.

Liberman, I. Y.; Shankweiler, D.; Fischer, F. W.; and Carter, B. 1974. Explicit syllable and phoneme segmentation in the young child. *Journal of Experimental Child Psychology* 18:201–12.

Lindamood, C. H., and Lindamood, P. C. 1975. *The A.D.D. Program, Auditory Discrimination in Depth*. Hingham, Mass.: Teaching Resources.

Lundberg, I.; Frost, J.; and Petersen, O-P. 1988. Effects of an extensive program for stimulating phonological awareness in preschool children. *Reading Research Quarterly* 23 (3): 263–84.

Lundberg, I.; Olofsson, A.; and Wall, S. 1980. Reading and spelling skills in the first school years, predicted from phonemic awareness skills in kindergarten. *Scandinavian Journal of Psychology* 21:159–73.

Magnusson, E., and Naucler, K. 1987. Language disordered and normally speaking children's development of spoken and written language: Preliminary results from a longitudinal study. *Reports from Uppsala University, Linguistics Department* 16:35–63.

Mann, V.; Liberman, I. Y.; and Shankweiler, D. 1980. Children's memory for sentences and word strings in relation to reading ability. *Memory and Cognition* 8:329–35.

Mann, V.; Shankweiler, D.; and Smith, S. 1984. The association between comprehension of spoken sentences and early reading ability: The role of phonetic representation. *Journal of Child Language* 11:627–43.

de Manrique, A. M. B., and Gramigna, S. 1984. La segmentacion fonologica y silabica en ninos de preescolar y primer grado. *Lectura y Vida* 5:4–13.

Marcel, A. 1980. Phonological awareness and phonological representation: Investigation of a specific spelling problem. In *Cognitive processes in spelling,* ed. U. Frith. London: Academic Press.

Mattingly, I. G. 1972. Reading, the linguistic process, and linguistic awareness. In *Language by Ear and by Eye: The Relationships between Speech and Reading,* ed. J. F. Kavanagh and I. G. Mattingly. Cambridge, Mass.: MIT Press.

Morais, J.; Cary, L.; Alegria, J.; and Bertelson, P. 1979. Does awareness of speech arise spontaneously? *Cognition* 7:323–31.

Morais, J.; Cluytens, M.; and Alegria, J. 1984. Segmentation abilities of dyslexics and normal readers. *Perceptual and Motor Skills* 58:221–22.

Olofsson, A., and Lundberg, I. 1983. Can phonemic awareness be trained in kindergarten? *Scandinavian Journal of Psychology* 24: 35–44.

Perfetti, C. A., and Goldman, S. R. 1976. Discourse memory and reading comprehension skill. *Journal of Verbal Learning and Verbal Behavior* 14:33–42.

Perfetti, C. A., and Lesgold, A. M. 1979. Coding and comprehension in skilled reading and implications for reading instruction. In *Theory and Practice of Early Reading,* vol. 1, ed. L. B. Resnick and P. A. Weaver. Hillsdale, N.J.: Erlbaum.

Pflaum, S. W.; Walberg, H. J.; Karegianes, M. L.; and Rasher, S. P. 1980. Reading instruction: A quantitative analysis. *Educational Research* 9:12–18.

Pratt. A. 1985. The relationship of linguistic awareness to reading skill in children and adults. Ph.D. diss., University of Rhode Island.

Read, C. 1986. *Children's Creative Spelling.* London: Routledge and Kegan Paul.

Read, C. and Ruyter, L. 1985. Reading and spelling skills in adults of low literacy. *Reading and Special Education* 6:43–52.

Savin, H. 1972. What the child knows about speech when he starts to learn to read. In *Language by Ear and by Eye: The Relationships between Speech and Reading,* ed. J. F. Kavanagh and I. G. Mattingly. Cambridge, Mass.: MIT Press.

Shankweiler, D., and Crain, S. 1986. Language mechanisms and reading disorders: a modular approach. *Cognition* 24:139–68.

Shankweiler, D., and Liberman, I. Y. 1972. Misreading: A search for causes. In *Language by Ear and by Eye: The Relationships between Speech and Reading,* ed. J. F. Kavanagh and I. G. Mattingly. Cambridge, Mass.: MIT Press.

Shankweiler, D.; Liberman, I. Y.; Mark, L. S.; Fowler, C. A.; and Fischer, F. W. 1979. The speech code and learning to read. *Journal of Experimental Psychology: Human Learning and Memory* 5: 531–45.

Shankweiler, D.; Smith, S. T.; and Mann, V. 1984. Repetition and comprehension of spoken sentences by reading disabled children. *Brain and Language* 12:241–57.

Slingerland, B. H. 1971. *A Multisensory Approach to Language Arts for Specific Language Disability Children: A Guide for Primary Teachers.* Cambridge, Mass.: Educators Publishing Service.

Smith, F. 1971. *Understanding Reading: A Psycholinguistic Analysis of Reading and Learning to Read.* New York: Holt, Rinehart and Winston.

Smith, S. T.; Macaruso, P.; Shankweiler, D.; and Crain, S. Forthcoming. Syntactic comprehension in young poor readers. *Applied Psycholinguistics.*

Stanovich, K. E. 1982. Individual differences in the cognitive processes of reading: I. Word decoding. *Journal of Learning Disabilities* 15:449–572.

Stein, C. L.; Cairns, H. S.; and Zurif, E. B. 1984. Sentence comprehension limitations related to syntactic deficits in reading disabled children. *Applied Psycholinguistics* 5:305–22.

Studdert-Kennedy, M. 1987. The phoneme as a perceptuo-motor structure. In *Language Perception and Production,* ed. A. Allport, D. MacKay, W. Prinz, and E. Sheerer. London: Academic Press.

Treiman, R. A., and Baron, J. 1981. Segmental analysis ability: Development and relation to reading ability. In *Reading Research: Advances in Theory and Practice,* vol. 3, ed. G. E. MacKinnon and T. G. Walker. New York: Academic Press.

Vellutino, F. R. 1979. *Dyslexia: Theory and Research.* Cambridge, Mass.: MIT Press.

Vellutino, F. R., and Scanlon, D. 1987. Phonological coding, phonological awareness, and reading ability: Evidence from longitudinal and experimental study. *Merrill-Palmer Quarterly* 33 (3): 321–63.

Vernon, M. D. 1957. *Backwardness in Reading, a Study of Its Nature and Origin.* Cambridge: Cambridge University Press.

Wagner, R. K., and Torgesen, J. K. 1987. The nature of phonological processing in the acquisition of reading skills. *Psychological Bulletin* 101:192–212.

Waters, G. S.; Seidenberg, M. S.; and Bruck, M. 1984. Children's and adults' use of spelling-sound information in three reading tasks. *Memory and Cognition* 12:293–305.

CHAPTER 2
How Problems of Comprehension Are Related to Difficulties in Decoding

Donald Shankweiler

Abstract

Those who view reading difficulties from the standpoint of comprehension have often focused on a different set of problems than those whose standpoint is the identification of individual words. Nonetheless the two kinds of problems—word decoding and sentence understanding—may be connected in several ways, as Perfetti and his colleagues have appreciated. The question considered in this chapter is whether the major difficulties at the level of the word and at the level of the sentence (and larger units of text) could have a common source. The chapter proposes how difficulties at each level might stem from a deficit in phonological processing, and it counters some empirical challenges to this viewpoint with arguments based on recent research.

Résumé

Ceux qui étudient les problèmes de lecture au niveau de la compréhension et ceux qui les étudient au niveau de l'identification des mots individuels, ils ont souvent concentré sur un groupe de problèmes très différents. Néanmoins, les deux types de problèmes—le déchiffrement des mots et la compréhension des phrases—dont Perfetti et d'autres se sont rendus compte, peuvent être liés en plusieurs façons. La question adressée dans cet article, cèst s'il y a une source en commun entre les difficultés au niveau du mot et celles au niveau de la phrase (et des segments plus larges du texte). L'article propose que les difficultés à chaque niveau peuvent être causées par un déficit dans les procès phonologiques et il contrarie quelques défis empiriques à ce point du vue à l'aide d'arguments basés sur de nouvelles recherches.

Zusammenfassung

Wissenschaftler, die Leseschwierigkeiten vom Blickwinkel des Verstehens aus betrachten, beschäftigen sich oft mit anderen Problemen, als jene, die sich auf die Erkennung einzelner Worte konzentrieren. Diese beiden Probleme—Worterkennung und Verstehen ganzer Sätze—sind aber wahrscheinlich miteinander verbunden, wie Perfetti und seine Mitarbeiter gezeigt haben. Der vorliegende Artikel behandelt die Frage, ob die hauptsächlichen Schwierigkeiten auf dem Niveau des Wortes und des Satzes (oder längerer Texteinheiten) einen gemeinsamen Ursprung haben. Wir schlagen vor, dass Leseschwierigkeiten in beiden Fällen auf mangelhafte phonologische Verarbeitung zuruckzuführen sind. Empirische Daten, die gegen ein solches Konzept angeführt wurden, scheinen in Anbetracht von Ergebnissen aus unseren letzten Untersuchungen durchaus damit vereinbar zu sein.

Resumen

A menudo, el estudio de las dificultades en la lectura desde el punto de vista de la comprensión se ha concentrado en un conjunto de problemas diferente del estudio cuya perspectiva es la identificación de palabras individuales. Sin embargo, según han podido apreciar Perfetti y otros investigadores, estos dos tipos de problemas—la descodificación de palabras y la comprensión de oraciones—pueden estar relacionados de formas diversas. Este trabajo se ocupa de investigar si las principales dificultades a los niveles de la palabra y de la frase (así como de unidades de texto mayores) tienen una causa común. Indica de qué modo las dificultades existentes en cada uno de ambos niveles pueden derivar de un déficit en la capacidad de procesamiento fonológico, y responde a algunos desafíos empíricos a esta perspectiva con argumentos basados en investigaciones recientes.

Although many in the field of reading research now hold that the causes of reading difficulty are to be found in the language domain, there are significant divisions of opinion concerning where within language the difficulties lie. My purpose in this chapter is to examine these divisions, to explain why it matters how they are resolved, to ask what evidence is pertinent, and to indicate where it leads.

The problem of assigning causes to failures in reading comprehension brings the divisions quickly to the surface. In this regard, a complaint one sometimes hears from reading teachers is that children may fail to comprehend a sentence in text even when they manage to decode all the words it contains. Indeed, the persisting failure of some children to comprehend what they read despite their ability to identify the words has lent credence to the view that, in addition to the difficulties in word decoding that are so apparent in most poor readers, a second set of difficulties may also exist.

How can we best frame those problems of reading that extend beyond the level of the word and assess their contribution to reading disability? Could the problems of comprehension be derived from the same basic limitation that is responsible for word decoding difficulties? I will argue that by investigating how lower-level language abilities are coordinated in reading, we may be able to explain the difficulties at the sentence level in the same terms as the difficulties at the level of the word. In developing our approach to reading difficulties, my colleagues and I have been guided by the possibility that the entire symptom picture in reading disorder, including many comprehension difficulties, may stem from a deficit in phonological processing.

We are aware that some investigators of reading problems will protest that such an account would inevitably fly in the face of the facts. Accordingly, in this chapter I have chosen to concentrate on findings of research that have appeared incompatible with the view that a phonological processing deficit can explain all the difficulties experienced by poor readers. A reinterpretation of these recalcitrant findings is proposed in the light of new experimental results.

Word Decoding and Text Comprehension

First I must clarify what I mean by decoding. It is obvious that comprehending the meaning of sentences and the larger units of text depends on correct apprehension of the individual words. By decoding, I simply mean the process, still incompletely understood, by which the reader identifies the printed words of the text. I am assuming, however, in keeping with the discussion in earlier chapters, that it is an analytic process—that efficient procedures for word recognition recover the linguistic information that the orthography provides. All beginning readers have to learn to identify in print the thousands of words they already know in speech. To succeed at this, the beginner needs to discover that words are phonological structures and to discover how their structures are reflected in their spellings. That is to say, every beginning reader who would ultimately become a good reader must learn to decode. (The first chapter summarized the evidence that poor decoding skills reflect lack of phonological awareness in the disabled reader, and that this problem, in turn, is caused by a wider deficit in phonological processing).

If decoding is a necessary condition for reading, it is clearly not a sufficient condition. In order to comprehend printed matter the would-be reader must also understand how the words of the text function in sentences and how sentences function in paragraphs. That is, a successful reader must parse the component sentences and unpack the argument structure of the text as a whole. But beginning readers come to the task of reading with a great deal of knowledge of the language already in hand. Through experience with speech, they know how to construct grammatical sentences and how to interpret them. Therefore, it can be argued, as it has been in the words of Gough and Tunmer (1986) that "once the printed matter is decoded, the reader applies to the text exactly the same mechanisms which he or she would bring to bear on its spoken equivalent" (9). On this view, learning to decode is the only new thing a speaker of the language must acquire to become a reader. Consistent with this viewpoint is the fact that a substantial correlation is regularly found between measures of decoding skill and more global reading measures, including measures of comprehension.

Measures of decoding are obtained by having someone read unfamiliar words (and nonwords that are possible words). Several researchers report that in school children these measures account for about half the variance in other measures of reading ability (e.g., Perfetti and Hogaboam 1975; Shankweiler and Liberman 1972; Stanovich 1986; Stanovich, Cunningham, and Feeman 1984). Perfetti (1985) has shown that decoding skills continue to distinguish different levels of comprehension even among adults at the college level, particularly if speed measures are taken as well as measures of accuracy. Even in the early grades, some poor readers who would pass as adequate decoders on the accuracy measure, may, in fact, still be slow and inefficient in decoding. The consistent association between reading measures based on decoding and measures based on comprehension indicates that a beginning reader, to be sure, and sometimes a more experienced reader as well, may encounter comprehension problems due to difficulties in deciphering the words of the text.

Is decoding, then, the only hurdle in learning to read? Some researchers think not, pointing to the existence of "hyperlexic" children who supposedly can decode well and yet comprehend poorly. However, the comprehension problems of these children do not seem to be limited to reading; hyperlexics appear to lack the higher-level language skills required for understanding verbal material in any form (Healy 1982; Huttenlocher and Huttenlocher 1973). In any case, such children probably constitute only a small proportion of those with reading problems. It is evident that a much larger group of poor readers have problems *both* in decoding and comprehension. Concerning this larger group, it might be supposed that they are beset with at least two deficits, a deficit that impairs apprehension of the individual words and a further independent deficit that impairs their grammatical integration. It would be natural for anyone who believed this to conclude that remedial measures that are directed to the decoding problem would only affect one source of the problems in comprehension. The other source would remain untouched. My coworkers and I, however, have arrived at a different view of the matter. We see the comprehension problems as part and parcel of the difficulties in decoding.

In summary, researchers who agree that the underlying problems in cases of reading disability are in the language domain do not always agree on where within that domain the problems lie or on how many basic problems there are. These researchers divide roughly into two camps on the question of causation. One side supposes that more than one basic deficit must be hypothesized to account for the total symptom picture. The alternative, which I will argue for here, supposes that in at least one major syndrome of reading disability, all the problems of reading spring ultimately from the same source.

Importance of Assessing Comprehension of Spoken Language

To resolve the question, it is necessary to broaden the scope of the investigation of reading problems to include the assessment of spoken language. To make a valid assessment of reading ability, we must examine the reader's comprehension of *both* spoken language and print. Since a failure of comprehension in reading may or may not extend to speech, it is essential to assess comprehension of spoken material before attempting to interpret anyone's failure to comprehend the equivalent material in printed form.

A recent paper by Gough and Tunmer (1986) affirms this important methodological principle. In advancing a "simple theory" of reading, the authors maintain that by measuring only two variables, decoding skill and listening comprehension, we can effectively account for *all* of the variance in reading comprehension. Indeed, they claim that reading skill is adequately described as the product of decoding and listening comprehension. That claim will require a large amount of data to evaluate fully, but let us suppose the simple theory is true and that together these two factors and their product do account statistically for all the variation in global measures of reading ability. If so, many possible causes of reading disability can be ruled out, such as oculomotor and visual perceptual deficits, or a deficit in general analytic ability.

At the same time, the Gough-Tunmer formula can, in principle, explain deviations from the normal course of learning to read. For example, hyperlexics, as we saw, are high on decoding skill, but low on comprehension. Dyslexics, on the other hand, are defined as those poor readers who display the opposite pattern. In contrast, most poor readers arguably have difficulties both in orthographic decoding and in listening comprehension (see discussion later in this chapter). It is apparent, however, that only the decoding problem is specific to reading. If a child fails to understand a sentence in print that would be readily comprehended in spoken form, the failure with print can be considered a failure specifically in reading. But, on the other hand, if the sentence is not comprehended even in speech, then the failure to read the sentence with understanding is wholly predictable from that fact alone. It could hardly be viewed as reflecting a reading problem as such.

The simple theory appeals to those who view reading, as my colleagues and I do, as a bottom-up process with decoding at its core. Insofar as the theory maintains that decoding is a skill that every new reader who would attain mastery must learn, we heartily agree. But despite this virtue, the simple theory encounters a difficulty in explaining why the children who have decoding problems are so often the very same children who have difficulties in comprehension of spoken sentences. Because the simple theory leaves unexplored the possible causal connections between the factors that limit orthographic decoding and the factors that limit listening comprehension, it can offer no ready explanation for the frequent co-occurrence of both difficulties in poor readers. The theory seems therefore not to encompass the possibility that difficulties in decoding and comprehension may be expressions of a deficit at a single level of language.

The challenge of how to weigh the contribution of poor decoding, how to assess the possible impact of higher-level language deficiencies, and how to properly understand the connection between the two leads us beyond the stage of examining correlations between various measures of decoding skill and global measures of comprehension. To understand the basis of individual differences in each aspect of reading, we need a theory that identifies the components of reading and explains how they are connected with one another and how each one comes into being in the developing child. If we agree that reading is a language skill, it would follow that a theory of reading would have to specify which parts of the language apparatus are needed for reading and how they must be modified to accept print rather than speech as input. This brings us to an examination of learning to read within the larger context of the child's acquisition of spoken language. Building on the framework of theory and method set down in the preceding chapters, I will give an account of reading disability that explains how problems at the word level and the sentence level could stem from a deficit in phonological processing, a deficit that limits both the decoding of printed words in reading and the operations of working memory in the on-line processing of spoken language.

Here, as in the discussion by Crain (in this volume) on the general problem of explaining childrens' failures in language comprehension, it will pay us to distinguish between an account based on a missing structure and an account based on overloading a language processor. To illustrate the importance of that distinction for developing a causal explanation of reading difficulties, it will be helpful to review findings of pioneering research by Vogel (1975) on the language abilities of good and poor beginning readers.

The study by Vogel, unusually insightful and thorough for its time, attempted a comprehensive assessment of morphological and syntactic abilities in children who differed strongly on standard tests of reading comprehension. Because this study raises several of the issues that concern us throughout this chapter, it is worth examining the findings in some detail. First, good and poor readers were distinguished on some but not all of the language measures. Interpretation of intonation patterns appropriate for statements and questions, verbatim repetition of syntactically complex sentences, tests that require a subject to supply missing grammatical suffixes that mark agreement, and a pair of cloze tests in which the subject listens to text in which every nth word is deleted and is required to supply the missing word—each distinguished the reading groups. But also of interest are the tasks on which the groups did not differ. The normal readers and reading disabled children did not differ in accuracy of making grammaticality judgments, or on comprehension of spoken sentences as measured by a picture selection task. But, as Vogel notes, the latter measures had poor reliability and content deficiencies as well, so the failure to find differences between the groups, particularly on the picture selection test, cannot be given much weight.

Appreciating that working memory is a relevant factor in the performance of many language tests, Vogel asked whether the differences between the reader groups that did emerge would remain after contribution of the memory factor was removed statistically. Using scores on digit span and word list recall as covariates, she reevaluated the relation between the "syntax" tests and reading comprehension. The result of the reanalysis was a considerable shrinkage of the correlation between reading comprehension and some of the spoken language tasks. The correlations that showed the greatest shrinkage were with the sentence repetition task and the cloze tests. With the contribution of the storage component of working memory removed, cloze performance no longer distinguished the groups; the residual effect of sentence repetition remained significant, though at a reduced level. From this analysis, we discover that short-term retention accounted for much of the variance between the reading groups on some of the so-called syntactic measures. The additional measures that continue to distinguish the groups after the variance due to the memory test was removed are the tests of production of inflected forms and elicited sentence production. Whereas it is clear that these tests tap morphological abilities, it is doubtful that either can be regarded as a test of syntactic ability as such. Indeed, none of the three measures which most sharply distinguished reading disabled from normal readers—two tests requiring production of inflectional suffixes (the Berry-Talbott test and the "grammatical closure" test of the Illinois Test of Psycholinguistic Abilities) and the prosody perception test—could be viewed as a pure measure of syntactic ability. Instead, both tests primarily tap lower-level language abilities (phonological and morphological).[1]

Vogel's study underlines the difficulty of disentangling the contribution of limitations in phonological processing, as revealed in measures of working memory, and limitations of structural knowledge in understanding comprehension difficulties. As I will explain shortly, these factors are often confounded in tasks commonly used to assess comprehension. The main thrust of the research from our laboratory has been directed toward teasing them apart experimentally.

In the past decade, several investigations have focused on comprehension of spoken language by children with reading disability. Although not every study has found unequivocal evidence of differences between matched groups of good and poor readers (e.g., Vogel 1975; Shankweiler, Smith, and Mann 1984), several have found good readers significantly more accurate than age-matched poor readers in comprehension of some structures in spoken sentences (e.g., Byrne 1981; Mann, Shankweiler, and Smith 1984; Smith, Mann, and Shankweiler 1986). The finding that poor readers do not always comprehend spoken sentences as well as good readers lends support to the possibility that inadequate decoding skill is only one of the barriers to comprehension.

Two Hypotheses about the Causes of Comprehension Difficulties

Two hypotheses have been advanced to explain the difficulties in spoken language comprehension. Taken at face value, the difficulties that poor readers display in interpreting sentences containing complex syntactic structures seem to point to gaps in their structural knowledge. If syntactic structures were missing from their internal grammars, spoken language comprehension would suffer, not just reading. We have called this the "structural deficit hypothesis" (Crain and Shankweiler 1988).

But if we heed the lessons from earlier attempts to test comprehension of complex structures in young children, we would do well to hesitate before drawing firm conclusions about the causes of comprehension difficulties in poor readers. Two caveats should be mentioned. The first is a methodological point: when someone fails to comprehend a spoken sentence with a certain syntactic structure, we cannot, without further analysis, assign a cause to the failure. In chapter 5, it is shown why the data one obtains from a comprehension test are not self interpreting, and why—unless certain precautions are observed—we may be led unwittingly to the wrong conclusions about the source of comprehension difficulty in poor readers. A second caveat reflects assumptions about the structure of the language apparatus. Before we can interpret properly the results of tests intended to measure comprehension, we must appreciate that language understanding, whether of speech or of printed material, is the end result of a complex series of steps. If just one of the steps goes awry, the understanding may be affected. In presenting a model of the language understanding system, Crain (in this volume) gives reasons for supposing that linguistic information flows through a hierarchy of structures and processors; it is stressed that apprehending the meaning of language input depends on the unimpeded passage of phonological information to the higher-level syntactic and semantic components of the language apparatus.

A further reason for caution in attributing comprehension difficulties to a lag in acquiring the requisite grammatical knowledge is the speed with which children pick up their spoken language. Some researchers on language acquisition believe that almost all of the grammatical structures of the language are already in place by the time instruction in reading usually begins (e.g., see Crain and Fodor, forthcoming). Psycholinguistic studies have demonstrated that the acquisition of language is guided by powerful innate constraints that give rise to impressive uniformities in the course of language acquisition across wide differences in language experience (Wanner and Gleitman 1982). Normal children invariably produce spoken language without direct instruction, much as they learn to walk without being taught. The same can be said of their abilities to understand spoken language. Ordinarily, however, people have to be taught to read. From a biological standpoint, the human species has not evolved special machinery for the perception of print as has evolved for the perception and production of speech.

In view of these considerations, one could well question whether the problem underlying poor readers' comprehension difficulties is likely to be a delay in the acquisition of syntactic knowledge. An alternative hypothesis supposes that the necessary syntactic structures are in place before the child begins to learn to read, and that difficulties in comprehension, both in spoken language and in text, are caused by deficiencies in processing phonological structures. The idea that deficits at the phonological level may underlie all the symptoms of reading disability is supported by evidence reviewed elsewhere in this volume. In addition to their difficulties in attaining awareness of the phonological structure of words, reading disabled children have a variety of other problems that implicate deficient phonologic processing, including difficulties in naming, difficulties in speech perception and production, and special limitations in working memory. The phonological deficit hypothesis can explain, as I will later show, how these diverse symptoms may reflect a single underlying problem, and it also gives an account of why the affected individuals have difficulty acquiring adequate word decoding strategies. This hypothesis faces its greatest challenge, however, in accounting for comprehension disturbances of poor readers, particularly their difficulties in spoken language comprehension (Shankweiler and Crain 1986).

Experiments on Comprehension of Spoken Sentences by Good and Poor Readers

A review of the relevant research follows next. I will pursue the idea that a deficiency in phonological processing may be the underlying cause of comprehension problems in many poor readers, both in spoken language and in reading. This simplifying perspective on reading disability can prevail only if we can reject the possibility that there are two basic deficits, one at the phonological level and another at the syntactic and/or semantic levels. The following experiments are designed to test between these possibilities.

Sentences Containing Restrictive Relative Clauses

First to be examined are research studies that compare reader groups on comprehension of sentences containing relative clauses. The relative clause has received a good deal of attention, largely because several studies of language acquisition have found that it emerges late in the course of normal development (Sheldon 1974; Tavakolian 1981). The relative clause plays a key role in the sentence grammar: it is a construction that allows the embedding of one sentence within another. In relative clause sentences, reference must be established between a superficially empty noun phrase in the relative clause and its antecedent noun phrase in the main clause. Coreference relations are governed by constraints involving the abstract structural representation underlying the sentence. These constraints rule out certain coreference possibilities and thereby restrict the semantic interpretations that a sentence can be assigned.

The relative clause has also figured prominently in attempts to assess the grammatical abilities of poor readers (Byrne 1981; Stein, Cairns, and Zurif 1984). It has been claimed that poor readers often have difficulty understanding sentences containing relative clause constructions because of a critical gap in syntactic knowledge. But other interpretations of the difficulties can also be made. Hamburger and Crain (1982) studied very young children's comprehension of sentences containing relative clauses, and gave an account of the extrasyntactic difficulties these sentences may present under varying pragmatic constraints. Among other factors that might be mentioned, their account notes that relative clause sentences may present the perceiver with a problem in *sequencing*. Consider, for example, the following sentence:

The cat scratched the dog that jumped through the hoop.

The second clause denotes an action that ordinarily would *precede* the action denoted by the first clause. Hamburger and Crain found that many children who performed the correct actions associated with sentences like this one, often failed to act out the designated events in the same order as adults. Thus, many three and four year olds acted out the sentence by first making the cat scratch the dog, and then making the dog jump through the hoop. Older children and normal adults typically act out these events in the opposite order, even though this entails acting out the later-occurring relative clause *before* the main clause. Intuitively, this order of events seems conceptually

Problems of Comprehension Related to Decoding 49

correct since "the dog that jumped through the hoop" is what the cat scratched. But this order of acting out the clauses would require longer storage of the phonological record. It is possible that the observed difference between the preschool children, on the one hand, and older children and adults, on the other hand, reflects the impact of young children's limited phonological processing capacities on their working memory. (This possibility is considered at the end of the chapter.)

As the example shows, an account of why poor readers have more difficulty than good readers in understanding sentences containing relative clause constructions might also appeal to a phonological processing deficit rather than to a structural lag. To test between these proposals, Mann, Shankweiler, and Smith (1984) conducted an object manipulation experiment with third grade good and poor readers using sentences containing relative clauses. Four types of relative clause structure were tested. In order to assess performance on each type, vocabulary and sentence length were held constant. So, in the sample set below, the same ten words recur in each sentence of the set.

a) The sheep pushed the cat that jumped over the cow.
b) The sheep that pushed the cat jumped over the cow.
c) The sheep pushed the cat that the cow jumped over.
d) The sheep that the cat pushed jumped over the cow.

The syntax varies in two ways—in the place of attachment of the relative clause, whether it is at the subject node or the direct object node, and in the role of the missing noun phrase in the relative clause, which, again, may be either subject or object.

The study by Mann, Shankweiler, and Smith confirmed earlier claims that poor readers can have difficulties in comprehending complex sentences even when they are presented in spoken form. But in several respects the findings invite the inference that the poor readers' problems with these relative clause sentences reflect a deficit in processing and not the absence of critical structures from their internal grammars. First, it was found that the type of relative clause structure had a large effect on comprehensibility. Sentence types *a* and *d* evoked the greatest number of errors in all the subjects. These are structures that earlier research on younger normal children also identified as the most difficult (Tavakolian 1981). Second, the poor readers made more errors than good readers in comprehension of each of the four types of relative clause structure. But the poor readers did not appear to lack any type of relative clause structure entirely. In fact, their pattern of errors closely mirrored that of the good readers; they simply did less well on each sentence type. This similarity in pattern would be difficult to explain if it were the case that the poor readers lacked one or more of these structures in their internal grammars. Their overall poorer performance would seem to require an explanation in terms of a processing difficulty.

Additional support for the view that the poor readers' difficulties with relative clauses reflect processing factors comes from data on short-term recall that were obtained in the second phase of the experiment by Mann, Shankweiler, and Smith. On a later day the same relative clause sentences were presented to the subjects again, this time for immediate recall. The poor readers made significantly more recall errors than the good readers in keeping with earlier findings on sentence memory (e.g., Perfetti and Goldman 1976; Mann, Liberman, and Shankweiler 1980; Vogel 1975). As was pointed out by Liberman, Shankweiler, and Liberman (in this volume), the deficits poor readers display in working memory are material specific: they have shown up consistently when good and poor readers were tested on a variety of materials that lend themselves to verbal coding, including letter strings, random word strings, and sentences. Nonverbal tasks, such as memory for spatial position, human faces, or abstract designs, do not place the poor reader at a disadvantage (Katz, Shankweiler, and Liberman 1981; Liberman et al. 1982). Findings such as these, when taken together with the data by Mann, Shankweiler, and Smith (1984) on error patterns in comprehension tasks, suggested that phonological processing difficulties, through their impact on working memory, are responsible for poor readers' failures in comprehension of relative-clause sentences. Thus it is not necessary to assume that incomplete syntactic knowledge is the source of the problem.

This interpretation of the comprehension data, while plausible, was not yet fully substantiated. Challenges that had earlier been raised in the literature had not been entirely dispelled. The question of whether reading disabled children show delayed or deviant patterns of acquisition of relative clause structures was pursued by Stein, Cairns, and Zurif (1984). Using data obtained from an act-out task, their study compared the performance of normal and reading disabled children in interpreting several relative clause structures that were also investigated by Mann, Shankweiler, and Smith (1984). Adopting the theoretical standpoint of staged acquisition of grammatical structures, the authors invoke a procedure that putatively enables one to gauge the stage of a child's grammatical development (Hsu, Cairns, and Fiengo, 1985). The results, like those of Mann, Shankweiler, and Smith (1984), showed that skilled readers performed better than reading impaired subjects, and that the difference was most marked at high levels of linguistic complexity. Application of the metric of grammatical development to the findings led the authors to infer that reading disabled children can be characterized as syntactically deviant from their controls since good and poor readers differed in the order of difficulty of the three relative clause structures that were assessed.

Although these results confirm other indications that poor readers are often not the equals of good readers in performance on comprehension tasks, they do not necessarily mean that poor readers have a deficit in structural knowledge. As we have seen, it is arguable that poor readers do not generally fail to comprehend sentences because of syntactic complexity, as such, but rather because of heavy memory demands that are sometimes confounded with complexity (see Crain and Shankweiler 1988).

Perhaps the strongest support for the view that poor readers' difficulties with relative clauses reflect processing overload comes from a comprehension study by Smith, Macaruso, Shankweiler, and Crain (forthcoming). This experiment exploits an earlier discovery by Hamburger and Crain (1982) that preschool children's errors in comprehension of restrictive relative clauses are remarkably reduced if, in the design of the test materials, care is taken to meet the presuppositions that the test sentences may evoke. Use of a restrictive relative clause with the definite article often implies that there are at least two objects of a particular category present in the experimental work space, either as props, if the task is a manipulation task, or as pictured objects if the task is a picture-selection test (see example in the next paragraph). The fact that most preschool children (in the Hamburger and Crain study) produced and understood relative clause sentences when the presuppositions underlying their use were satisfied, suggests that failure to meet this requirement in previous studies interfered with children's comprehension of the test sentences. In the case of poor readers, the findings in the literature of impaired performance on comprehension of relative clause sentences might also be tied to excessive processing demands imposed by unmet presuppositions.

To explore this possibility, in the study by Smith et al. (forthcoming) two objects were made available in the experimental workspace to represent the head noun of the relative clause. For the sample sentence shown below, two sheep were placed in the experimental workspace, where only one had appeared in previous studies.

The sheep that the cat pushed jumped over the cow.

Presumptively, the extra sheep was *not* pushed by the cat and did *not* jump over the cow. With this change in place, Smith et al. compared their findings with those of the Mann, Shankweiler, and Smith (1984) study, in which the same subject selection criteria were used, but in which the presuppositions of relative clauses were not met. The data lend strong support to a processing limitation hypothesis. It was found that both good and poor readers made far fewer errors in the Smith et al. study, in which the pragmatic presuppositions of the restrictive relative clause were satisfied, than occurred in the experiment by Mann, Shankweiler, and Smith (1984) (despite the fact that the subjects of the latter investigation were nearly a year older).

It is apparent that the manipulations of Smith et al. permitted us to pose questions about the children's syntactic knowledge in a way that drastically reduced the nonsyntactic demands. By adopting a procedure that minimizes the processing requirements in a comprehension task, it was found that children with reading disability performed as well as good readers in many instances. We see, then, that the failure in previous work to control for nonsyntactic aspects of sentence comprehension tasks led to underestimates of the grammatical capabilities of reading disabled children. This also holds true of other grammatical constructions as well, as the following examples show.

Sentences Containing Temporal Terms

Sentences that make correct use of temporal terms, such as *before* and *after*, have been found to emerge late in the course of language development (Amidon and Carey 1972). The difficulties children encounter in comprehending temporal terms have been diversely explained in the literature. In keeping with the notion of a structural deficit is the proposal that temporal terms are mastered late because children lack certain structural knowledge that is essential to sentences with subordinate syntax. This interpretation gains support from the finding that children regularly encounter difficulty in acting out temporal term sentences such as *e*, which pose a conflict between order of mention and order of execution. This presents yet another instance of a sequencing problem, such as we examined earlier in certain relative clause sentences.

It is important to note that children do not have difficulty with sentences like *g*, which also pose a sequencing problem.

e) Push the motorcycle after you push the helicopter.
f) After you push the helicopter, push the motorcycle.
g) Push the motorcycle last; push the helicopter first.

Crain suggests that the earlier studies that evoked differential responses to *e* and *g* failed to control for a presupposition present in sentence *e*. The presupposition associated with this sentence is that the hearer intends to push the helicopter. To satisfy this presupposition, the subject's object preference must be established *before* the request in *e* is made. In keeping with this principle, Crain (1982) developed a procedure that requires subjects to establish their intent to perform the action mentioned in the clause introduced by the temporal term. On this procedure, children are asked, before each test sentence is presented, to identify one object they want to play with in the next part of the game. The experimenter subsequently incorporates this information in the subordinate clause introduced by the temporal term. So for example, sentence *e* would have been presented only after a subject had chosen to play with the helicopter, which pragmatically justifies the use of the temporal term (i.e., makes it "felicitous").

Crain has shown substantial gains in children's comprehension of sentences like *e* when the context was made meaningful by eliciting object preferences before testing. This would implicate processing demands, not lack of grammatical knowledge, as a possible reason for the difficulties such sentences pose when they are presented without contextual support. With this background in mind, we anticipated that both good and poor readers would display a high rate of successful comprehension of temporal terms sentences in felicitous contexts, but that the performance of poor readers would suffer in contexts that are not supportive (i.e., when the presupposition associated with the use of temporal terms is not satisfied). However, if the poor readers' difficulties with these sentences are the result of insufficient knowledge of structures, then poor performance should occur with or without contextual support.

We have recently completed a study of good and poor readers' comprehension of sentences containing the temporal terms *before* and *after* (Macaruso et al., forthcoming). Four sentences were presented in which the order of mention of events was the same as the order of execution, as in *f*. In the remaining twelve sentences, order of mention was opposite to the order of execution, as in *e*. As noted above, the sentences were presented both with contextual support (i.e., with object preference preestablished before each test trial) and without contextual support.

Poor readers performed less well overall than good readers in acting out these temporal terms sentences. In addition, the inclusion of contextual support resulted in a significant reduction of errors for both groups. In fact, the poor readers benefited more from the provision of context than the good readers. Poor readers performed with a success rate of 82 percent when the presupposition associated with temporal terms was satisfied. This outcome does not sit well with the syntactic lag hypothesis.

The findings of this experiment indicate that as processing demands are increased, poor readers' performance involving temporal terms is degraded to a greater extent than good readers. Decreasing processing demands by satisfying presuppositions elevates performance of the poor readers to a greater extent than the good readers such that group differences diminish and both reader groups perform with a high level of accuracy.

Detection and Correction of
Grammatical Anomalies

In a further attempt to disentangle syntactic knowledge and processing capabilities in beginning readers, Fowler (1988) assessed spoken sentence understanding by means of a task that minimizes processing demands: judgment of sentence grammaticality. The grammaticality judgment task was considered the best available measure of syntactic competence. This expectation is motivated in part by recent research on aphasia which has shown that agrammatic aphasic patients with severe memory limitations were able to detect grammatical violations in sentences of considerable length and syntactic complexity (Shankweiler, Crain, Gorrell, and Tuller, forthcoming; Linebarger, Schwartz, and Saffran 1983). The findings from aphasia suggest that this task directly taps the syntactic analysis that is assigned.

In addition, Fowler required her subjects to change the ungrammatical sentences in a way that makes them grammatical. The correction task is far more demanding of memory resources than the judgment task. Correcting grammatical anomalies requires the ability to hold sentence in memory long enough for reanalysis.

According to the phonological deficit hypothesis, both good and poor readers should do equally well on the judgment task, but differences between the groups should emerge on the correction task. This was indeed what was found. Reading ability was significantly correlated with success on the correction task, but not with success on the judgment task (in keeping with findings of Vogel 1975, discussed earlier). This result must surely be viewed as support for the hypothesis that processing complexity, and not syntactic complexity as such, is the basis of the comprehension difficulties in poor readers. Further support for this inference comes from the additional finding that results on a test of short-term recall (with the influence of IQ removed) were more strongly correlated with success on the sentence correction task than with success on the judgment task.

Together, the studies we have reviewed confirm the indications of earlier research that poor beginning readers often have significant difficulties in comprehending some spoken sentences. But our research leads us to reject the idea that a syntactic lag is the basis of these comprehension problems. The syntactic lag hypothesis cannot explain the pattern of findings that emerge from these studies. It cannot explain why reader group differences sometimes disappear completely when the critical structures are presented in a way that minimizes processing load, nor can it explain the fact that performance with these structures varies up or down depending on task complexity.

A Phonological Deficit Unites the Difficulties in Comprehension with Those in Decoding

In summary, we have shown how the obtained differences between the reading groups can be explained on the processing limitation hypothesis. First, it was shown that relative clause structures present the same difficulties for reading disabled children as they do for other children, and that the source of the difficulty certain of these sentences pose is pragmatic and procedural, not syntactic. Further, many of the structures that children find most difficult are those that present a problem of sequencing and therefore require the subject to retain the first mentioned clause while acting out the second. It is proposed that poor readers are more limited than normal readers in the memory resources needed to retain phonological information in memory while the correct ordering of events is worked out. That is why we argue that poor readers are particularly prone to error on these sentences (Crain et al., forthcoming). Accordingly, when the experimental context is controlled to minimize processing load, poor readers improve dramatically, sometimes performing as well as good readers (see Smith et al., forthcoming).

A similar line of argument was made for sentences containing temporal terms. Here, too, the difficulty could arise either from syntactic complexity as such or from processing difficulties attendant upon that complexity. It was argued that the difficulties that such sentences present arise, again, largely from the problem of sequencing and the attendant demands on memory. The requirement for retention of phonological information is greater still in the correction task employed by Fowler.

This chapter began with the observation that for some researchers, the problems poor readers evince in decoding words must be explained in different terms than are used to explain their problems in understanding sentences. The first problem appears on the surface to be quite specific to reading: poor readers cannot successfully make analytic use of the orthography to recover the words of the text. The second problem is apparently broader: poor readers also have difficulties in processing higher-level linguistic information in some sentences, even in spoken language.

Appearances may deceive us, however. The results we have obtained lead us to conclude that *neither* problem is entirely specific to reading—not the problem at the level of the word nor the problem at the level of the sentence. Reading disabled children have difficulties in setting up and using phonological structures and, as is seen throughout this volume, these difficulties manifest themselves in a variety of ways. One manifestation is in the development of decoding skills. Other chapters in this volume examine the evidence that underlying the difficulties in learning to decode, there are a host of phonological deficiencies, some rather subtle, which are revealed through use of appropriate spoken language tasks. Deficits in phonological processing can explain the difficulties poor readers typically experience in learning how to use the orthography. Less obviously, deficits arising from this source can explain poor readers' problems in comprehension, both in reading and in spoken language, as consequences of their effects on working memory.

Having shown by experiments that the syntactic deficit hypothesis cannot in these instances explain the difficulties that poor readers display in comprehension of spoken sentences, we should indicate what considerations lead us to assert that the comprehension problems are a manifestation of phonological processing deficiencies that limit the normal operations of working memory. It must be acknowledged that direct empirical support for this proposal is so far rather limited. So far, few children have been thoroughly studied on both phonological processing tasks and comprehension tasks. But there is another ingredient needed in order to give foundation to a comprehensive theory of reading disability: it will be necessary to amplify and extend the notion of working memory and to explain how the operations of working memory depend on the integrity of phonological processes.

Memory is an essential part of language processing, because language is by its nature sequential: a linguistic message unfolds over time. The pioneering studies of Conrad (1964) and Baddeley (1966) showed that when verbal material, whatever its source, is maintained by rehearsal, the errors reflect phonological properties of the items, rather than some other properties, such as their semantic characteristics. This research led to the general conclusion that the memory system required for integration of words into sentences and larger units of text or discourse relies critically on phonological processes.

An important further development that led to the concept of working memory was stimulated by the need to show how memory is actually used in language processing. An important step in this direction was taken by Baddeley and Hitch (1974) and Daneman and Carpenter (1980), who argued convincingly that the memory system involved in on-line comprehension is not just a storage bin but an operational device. Perfetti and his colleagues have expressed similar views (Perfetti and Goldman 1976; Perfetti 1985). In addition to its storage function, the working memory system also incorporates a control function. In recent papers, several colleagues and I have developed a proposal about how working memory operates in processing spoken language and print (Crain et al., forthcoming; Shankweiler and Crain 1986; Shankweiler, Crain, Brady, and Macaruso, forthcoming). The following is a brief summary of conclusions presented in those papers. As is pointed out in the chapter by Crain (in this volume), the primary function of the control component is to regulate the flow of linguistic information through the interlocking system of parsers. On this proposal, it is the duty of working memory to transfer linguistic information from one component to another of the general language understanding system. That is, one of the jobs of working memory is to transfer phonologically analyzed material out of the limited memory store and push it upward to the syntactic processor, at the same time freeing the storage area to accept the next chunk of phonological material.

Our view of working memory, like the views of others mentioned above, attributes to it both processing and storage functions. Our proposal, however, differs in fundamental ways from other models in the literature. In keeping with the assumption of the modular organization of the lanaguage apparatus, we conceive of verbal working memory as a specialized device that specifically serves the language apparatus. This distinguishes our proposal from those by Baddeley (1986) and Carpenter and Just (1988). These researchers see working memory as a general purpose device that plays a central role not only in language, but also in problem solving, spatial reasoning, and other diverse forms of complex thinking.

Applying our working memory model to the spoken language comprehension problems of poor readers, we suggested why certain structures are particularly vulnerable to comprehension failure. We explained that many sentences containing relative clauses and some sentences containing temporal terms present a sequencing problem. In the most difficult of these, the clauses have to be acted out in the reverse of their order of arrival. Such sentences exact a heavy toll on working memory because the first clause has to be stored while the second clause is being processed and must remain in storage until a decision is reached about what action is to be performed first. But, as noted, the costs to memory can be reduced by changes in the testing procedure, and it is important that these procedural changes consistently reduced the performance gap between good and poor readers. Thus, the value of this conception of working memory for the analysis of language comprehension problems is that it allows us to make fairly specific predictions about the sentences that will be most costly of memory resources, and, accordingly, will cause the greatest difficulty for anyone with a deficit in phonological processing.

It should be apparent that working memory, on this view, cannot be tested by rote recall tests alone. These tap only the storage component of the system. It has been found, not surprisingly if our view of the complex nature of working memory is correct, that recall measures are sometimes only weakly correlated with measures of reading skill (Daneman and Carpenter 1980). Unfortunately, recall measures are mainly what are available to us in studies comparing good and poor readers.

How Decoding Affects Comprehension

Other things equal, a limitation of working memory stemming from a phonological deficit would have a greater impact on reading than on spoken language comprehension. In spoken language, the phonological structures are extracted from the acoustic signal by the innate speech apparatus that evolution has fashioned to do just that job. But in reading the phonologic information that serves as input to working memory has to be extracted by orthographic decoding routines that, until highly practiced, are inaccurate and slow. In the poor reader, decoding skills remain inadequate as a consequence of their deficiencies in the phonological abilities on which the development of these skills depend.

It is easy to see, on this view, why unskilled decoding is so regularly associated with poor comprehension. The association can be explained on the hypothesis that when the individual words of a text are read too slowly (even if accurately), comprehension suffers because the integrative processes are disturbed. The memory system that is used both in speech understanding and in reading cannot store many discrete items, especially if their order of arrival must be retained. The system can hang on to about five to seven unrelated words before it begins to lose some of them (Miller 1956). Moreover, this form of memory has a very limited survival time; unorganized material can be retained for only a few seconds without continuous rehearsal. Excessively slow decoding constricts the working memory system in failing to recover the phonological segments rapidly enough to permit the sentence parser to function efficiently. Perfetti and Lesgold (1977, 1979) proposed that if the limited working memory resources are used up on getting to the words of the text, there will be insufficient resources left over to support higher-level language processes.

In reading, the transfer of information into and out of the memory store is limited by the level of word decoding skill. If the level of skill is low, all higher-level processes will be depressed. In the worst case, even the simplest sentences would not be understood. But at intermediate levels of decoding skill, somewhere between the state of the rank beginner and the fluent experienced reader, there will be a gap between what can be understood in print and in spoken form. Unless and until the gap is closed, some sentences will cause more difficulty in print than in spoken form. These are the sentences that, for reasons we have considered, often require reanalysis.

Thus we can readily appreciate the connection between poor decoding and poor comprehension when we see that phonological processing limitations create a kind of bottleneck that limits the assimilation of lower-level language structures into higher-level ones. Because working memory has a small capacity and decays rapidly, it must receive new material at a rate that is neither too fast nor too slow in order to function well in language understanding. Everyone has experienced the difficulties of listening to speech when there are inappropriate pauses between every word. By the time the end of the sentence is reached, the earlier words have faded. Now consider what we know about the unskilled reader. In reading, the decoder works haltingly, in fits and starts. As Perfetti and Lesgold have stressed, the slow rate of input hobbles working memory and creates the bottleneck in moving from words to sentences. Therefore, the meaning is often lost. That, presumably, is the reason why decoding test measures and comprehension test measures are usually significantly associated with one another.

If, as Gough and Tunmer contend, *all* of the variance in reading is attributable jointly to orthographic decoding and listening comprehension, then if variations in each factor stem from the same source, as we have argued, we are in a position to tie together the whole range of difficulties that research finds associated with reading disability. These include difficulties in attaining awareness of phonological segments with attendant failure to grasp the alphabetic principle; difficulties that special testing may bring to light in speech perception, speech production, and naming; and difficulties in managing the working memory on which comprehension both in reading and spoken language depends. Together these symptoms form a syndrome. Each symptom can be regarded as a manifestation of weakness in processing the phonological structures of language (see Crain et al., forthcoming; Liberman and Shankweiler 1985; Shankweiler and Crain 1986).

Why Does It Matter?

An emphasis on decoding in the teaching of beginning reading is natural to those who, like the researchers represented in this volume, think of reading as proceeding essentially in a bottom-up fashion: identifying the words of the text, and their constituent phonological segments, is a necessary prerequisite to comprehending the sentences and the larger units. This perspective, we have maintained, allows reading to share much of the apparatus for spoken language (see Shankweiler and Crain 1986; Shankweiler and Liberman 1976). Once the neophyte reader has constructed new procedures for identifying words in their orthographically coded form, the other parts of the language apparatus could conceivably be taken over intact. Well before the child's first day at school, the higher-level abilities, such as syntax, are already in place and regularly in use in understanding and producing spoken language.

How we view poor readers' failures in comprehension determines the recommendations we make for prevention and treatment of reading problems. If we fail to appreciate the central role decoding plays in reading, we may easily mistake a lower-level processing deficit for a sign of a missing grammatical structure. If we wrongly attribute children's failures to the absence of certain complex syntactic structures, other mistakes may follow: We may be led to make unnecessary text simplifications that rob the language of its vitality and lead to boredom (see Crain and Shankweiler 1988). But if we are correct in our diagnosis that failures in comprehension can often be attributed to limitations of working memory resources stemming from deficits in phonological processing, we can take appropriate steps to reduce the processing demands of reading texts. These steps would include provision of contextual supports for satisfying the child's presuppositions and scrupulous application to children's reading materials of standards of clarity and style (see Bolinger 1965) that afford protection against the insipidities of "Dick and Jane" primers.

What direct remedial measures can be taken to boost the slow reader? Evidence was reviewed in chapter 1 that the phonological segmentation abilities that underlie word decoding can be successfully taught at any age. Since weaknesses in processing lower-level components in the language hierarchy have important repercussions at higher levels, our first priority must be to strengthen decoding and through practice to develop fluency in recognizing printed words. These measures should do more than anything else to improve reading comprehension by enabling the poor reader to use limited working memory resources efficiently. Only when facility with word identification is attained can the working memory system be used effectively to gain access to syntactic, semantic, and pragmatic structures.

As noted at the outset, it is often argued that an effective approach to research on reading disorders and their treatment must be concerned not only with the problems of learning to read words, but also with comprehension. Taking this concern at face value, it would be hard to disagree. The goal of reading, after all, is to comprehend what is written. Too often, however, an expressed concern with comprehension signals a wish to downplay the importance of decoding. The slogan "reading for meaning" has become a bandwagon on which all the opponents of approaches that emphasize decoding have climbed. The slogan and the polemics that surround it have had an unfortunate result. They have fostered the assumption that an approach to reading that emphasizes comprehension is necessarily at odds with one that emphasizes decoding. A major purpose in writing this chapter was to dispel that misconception and to show that a genuine concern with what limits reading comprehension leads us back to decoding difficulties and their causes.

NOTES

The research discussed in this chapter was supported in part by a Program Project Grant to Haskins Laboratories from the National Institute of Child Health and Human Development (HD-01994). I am grateful to Stephen Crain, Isabelle Y. Liberman, and Paul Macaruso for much valuable discussion and for their insightful comments on earlier drafts.

1. Vogel attempted also to assess which of her language tests were the best predictors of reading comprehension. Unfortunately, the regression analysis designed to answer this question obscures some things that are potentially important because (for purposes of the analysis) the language tests were grouped in such a way that the predictive value of each individual test cannot be assessed independently. Vogel's findings, while generally in accord with other research on the determinants of reading comprehension, are deviant in failing to confirm the predictive value of decoding.

REFERENCES

Amidon, A., and Carey, P. 1972. Why five-year-olds cannot understand *before* and *after*. *Journal of Verbal Learning and Verbal Behavior* 11:417–23.

Baddeley, A. D. 1966. Short-term memory for word sequences as a function of acoustic, semantic and formal similarity. *Quarterly Journal of Experimental Psychology* 18:362–65.

———. 1986. *Working Memory*. Oxford: Oxford University Press.

Baddeley, A. D., and Hitch, G. B. 1974. Working memory. In *The Psychology of Learning and Motivation*, vol. 8, ed. G. H. Bower. New York: Academic Press.

Bolinger, D. 1965. Maneuvering for accent and position. In *Forms of English Accent, Morpheme, Order*, ed. I. Abe and T. Kanekiyo. Cambridge, Mass.: Harvard University Press.

Byrne, B. 1981. Deficient syntactic control in poor readers: Is a weak phonetic memory code responsible? *Applied Psycholinguistics* 2: 201–12.

Carpenter, P. A., and Just, M. A. 1988. The role of working memory in language comprehension. In *The Impact of Herbert A. Simon*, ed. D. Klahr and K. Kotovsky. Hillsdale, N.J.: Erlbaum.

Conrad, R. 1964. Acoustic confusions in immediate memory. *British Journal of Psychology* 3:75–84.

Crain, S. 1982. Temporal terms: Mastery by age five. In *Papers and Reports on Child Language Development,* vol. 21. Stanford: Stanford University.

Crain, S, and Fodor, J. D. Forthcoming. Competence and performance in child language. In *Language and Cognition: A Developmental Perspective,* ed. E. Dromi. Norwood, N. J.: Ablex.

Crain, S., and Shankweiler, D. 1988. Syntactic complexity and reading acquisition. In *Linguistic Complexity and Text Comprehension: Readability Issues Reconsidered,* ed. A. Davison, and G. Green. Hillsdale, N. J.: Erlbaum.

Crain, S.; Shankweiler, D.; Macaruso, P.; and Bar-Shalom, E. Forthcoming. Working memory and sentence comprehension: Investigations of children with reading disorder. In *Neuropsychological Impairments of Short-Term Memory,* ed. G. Vallar and T. Shallice. Cambridge: Cambridge University Press.

Daneman, M., and Carpenter, P. A. 1980. Individual differences in working memory and reading. *Journal of Verbal Learning and Verbal Behavior* 19:450–66.

Fowler, A. 1988. Grammaticality judgments and reading skill in Grade 2. *Annals of Dyslexia* 38:73–94.

Gough, P. B., and Tunmer, W. E. 1986. Decoding, reading and reading disability. *Remedial and Special Education* 7:6–10.

Hamburger, H., and Crain, S. 1982. Relative acquisition. In *Language Development,* vol. 1, *Syntax and Semantics,* ed. S. Kuczaj. Hillsdale, N.J.: Erlbaum.

Healy, J. M. 1982. The enigma of hyperlexia. *Reading Research Quarterly* 17:319–38.

Hsu, J. R.; Cairns, H. S.; and Fiengo, R. W. 1985. The development of grammar underlying children's interpretation of complex sentences. *Cognition* 20:25–48.

Huttenlocher, R. R., and Huttenlocher, J. A. 1973. A study of children with hyperlexia. *Neurology* 23:1107–16.

Katz, R. B.; Shankweiler, D.; and Liberman, I. Y. 1981. Memory for item order and phonetic recoding in the beginning reader. *Journal of Experimental Child Psychology* 32:474–84.

Liberman, I. Y.; Mann, V. A.; Shankweiler, D.; and Werfelman, M. 1982 Children's memory for recurring linguistic and nonlinguistic material in relation to reading ability. *Cortex* 18:367–75.

Liberman, I. Y., and Shankweiler, D. 1985. Phonology and the problems of learning to read and write. *Remedial and Special Education* 6:8–17.

Linebarger, M., Schwartz, M., and Saffran, E. M. 1983. Sensitivity to

grammatical structure in so-called agrammatic aphasia. *Cognition* 13:361–92.
Macaruso, P.; Bar-Shalom, E.; Crain, S.; and Shankweiler, D. Forthcoming. Comprehension of temporal terms by good and poor readers. *Language and Speech* 32.
Mann, V. A.; Liberman, I. Y.; and Shankweiler, D. 1980. Children's memory for sentences and word strings in relation to reading ability. *Memory and Cognition* 8:329–35.
Mann, V. A.; Shankweiler, D.; and Smith, S. T. 1984. The association between comprehension of spoken sentences and early reading ability: The role of phonetic representation. *Journal of Child Language* 11:627–43.
Miller, G. A. 1956. The magical number seven, plus or minus two, or, some limits on our capacity for processing information. *Psychological Review* 63:81–96.
Perfetti, C. A. 1985. *Reading Ability.* New York: Oxford University Press.
Perfetti, C. A., and Goldman, S. R. 1976. Discourse memory and reading comprehension skill. *Journal of Verbal Learning and Verbal Behavior* 14:33–42.
Perfetti, C. A., and Hogaboam, T. 1975. The relationship between single word decoding and reading comprehension skill. *Journal of Educational Psychology* 67:461–69.
Perfetti, C. A., and Lesgold, A. M. 1977. Discourse comprehension and sources of individual differences. In *Cognitive Processes in Comprehension,* ed. M. A. Just and P. A. Carpenter. Hillsdale, N.J.: Erlbaum.
———. 1979. Coding and comprehension in skilled reading and implications for reading instruction. In *Theory and Practice of Early Reading,* ed. L. B. Resnick and P. Weaver. Hillsdale, N.J.: Erlbaum.
Shankweiler, D., and Crain, S. 1986. Language mechanisms and reading disorders: A modular approach. *Cognition* 24:139–68.
Shankweiler, D.; Crain, S.; Brady, S.; and Macaruso, P. Forthcoming. Identifying the causes of reading disability. In *Reading Acquisition,* ed. P. B. Gough. Hillsdale: N.J.: Erlbaum.
Shankweiler, D.; Crain, S.; Gorrell, P.; and Tuller, B. Forthcoming. Reception of language in Broca's aphasia. *Language and Cognitive Processes.*
Shankweiler, D., and Liberman, I. Y. 1972. Misreading: A search for causes. In *Language by Ear and by Eye: The Relationships between Speech and Reading,* ed. J. F. Kavanagh and I. G. Mattingly. Cambridge, Mass.: MIT Press.

———. 1976. Exploring the relations between reading and speech. In *The Neuropsychology of Learning Disorders,* ed. R. M. Knights, and D. J. Bakker. Baltimore, Md.: University Park Press.

Shankweiler, D.; Smith, S. T.; and Mann, V. A. 1984. Repetition and comprehension of spoken sentences by reading-disabled children. *Brain and Language* 23:241–57.

Sheldon, A. 1974. The role of parallel function in the acquisition of relative clauses in English. *Journal of Verbal Learning and Verbal Behavior* 13:272–81.

Smith, S. T.; Macaruso, P.; Shankweiler, D.; and Crain, S. Forthcoming. Syntactic comprehension in young poor readers. *Applied Psycholinguistics.*

Smith, S. T.; Mann, V. A.; and Shankweiler, D. 1986. Spoken sentence comprehension by good and poor readers: A study with the Token Test. *Cortex* 22:627–32.

Stanovich, K. E. 1986. Matthew effects in reading: Some consequences of individual differences in the acquisition of literacy. *Reading Research Quarterly* 21:360–407.

Stanovich, K. E.; Cunningham, A. E.; and Feeman, D. J. 1984. Intelligence, cognitive skills and early reading progress. *Reading Research Quarterly* 19:278–301.

Stein, C. L.; Cairns, H. S.; and Zurif, E. B. 1984. Sentence comprehension limitations related to syntactic deficits in reading-disabled children. *Applied Psycholinguistics* 5:305–22.

Tavakolian, S. L. 1981. The conjoined-clause analysis of relative clauses. In *Language Acquisition and Linguistic Theory,* ed. S. Tavakolian. Cambridge, Mass.: MIT Press.

Vogel, S. A. 1975. *Syntactic Abilities in Normal and Dyslexic Children.* Baltimore, Md.: University Park Press.

Wanner, E., and Gleitman, L. R. 1982. Language acquisition: The state of the state of the art. In *Language Acquisition: The State of the Art,* ed. E. Wanner and L. R. Gleitman. Cambridge: Cambridge University Press.

CHAPTER 3
Phonology and Reading: Evidence from Profoundly Deaf Readers

Vicki L. Hanson

Abstract

The prelingually, profoundly hearing-impaired reader of English is at an immediate disadvantage in that he or she must read an orthography that was designed to represent the phonological structure of English. Can the deaf reader become aware of this structure in the absence of significant auditory input? Evidence from studies with deaf college students will be considered. These studies indicate that successful deaf readers do appreciate the phonological structure of words and that they exploit this knowledge in reading. The finding of phonological processing by these deaf readers makes a strong case for the importance of phonological sensitivity in the acquisition of skilled reading, whether in hearing readers or deaf readers.

Résumé

Le lecteur d'anglais qui à subi une perte d'audition avant le début de sa capacité de parler a un désavantage immédiat en ce qu'il est obligé de lire une orthographie dessinée à représenter la structure phonologique de l'anglais. Est-il possible que ce lecteur sourd puisse devenir conscient de cette structure dans l'absence de signaux auditoires assez forts? On considérera l'évidence obtenu dans des études avec des étudiants universitaires sourds. Ces études indiquent que les lecteurs sourds qui réussissent, se rendent compte de la structure phonologique des mots et qu'ils utilisent cette information pour lire et pour écrire. L'évidence des procès phonologiques chez ces lecteurs sourds recommande beaucoup l'importance de la sensibilité phonologique en l'acquisition de la lecture, soit chez ceux qui entendent bien, soit chez ceux qui sont sourds.

Zusammenfassung

Englisch-sprechende Personen, die ihr Gehör vor dem Spracherwerb verloren, sind beim Lesen benachteiligt, da die englische Orthographie phonologische Struktur darstellt. Können gehörlose Leser diese Struktur erkennen, die gesprochene Sprache charakterisiert? Experimente an gehörlosen Studenten zeigen, daß erfolgreiche Leser die phonologische Wortstruktur erkennen und dieses Wissen im Lesen und Schreiben ausnützen. Diese Resultate unterstützen die in der Forschung mit normal hörenden Kindern entwickelte Hypothese, daß phonologische Analyse wichtig für das Erlernen des Lesens ist.

Resumen

Desde su infancia, el lector de inglés severamente incapacitado para la audición se encuentra en desventaja con relación a la lectura de la ortografía utilizada para representar la estructura fonológica del inglés. Dada su incapacidad auditiva, ¿puede el lector sordo llegar a comprender aquella estructura? Para elucidar esta cuestión tomaremos en consideración datos reportados en estudios que tratan sobre estudiantes sordos de enseñanza secundaria. Estos estudios indican que los lectores sordos aventajados aprecian la estructura fonológica de las palabras, y que utilizan este conocimiento en la lectura y en la escritura. El hecho de que estos lectores sordos puedan procesar un mensaje fonológicamente prueba claramente la importancia de la sensibilidad fonológica en la adquisición de la capacidad de lectura, tanto en el caso de las personas que oyen como de las incapacitadas para la audición.

In the normal course of events, children are fluent speakers and listeners of their native tongue, English, before they begin learning to read. In this chapter, I am concerned with a population of readers for whom this is not the case. This population is prelingually, profoundly hearing impaired. For these deaf readers, speech and lipreading are difficult to acquire and require years of instruction.

Research on reading has indicated that building on a spoken language foundation is a critical feature of reading and that in order to use an alphabetic orthography, such as English, to best advantage, the reader must go beyond the visual shape of words to apprehend their internal phonological structures (Liberman 1971, 1973). Despite their extensive experience in using the phonology in everyday speech, evidence presented elsewhere in this monograph argues that hearing children who are poor readers may have phonological deficits that underlie their reading problems. These children have difficulty in setting up phonological structures, in apprehending such structures in words, and in using a phonetic code for the storage and processing of words in working memory. The phonological deficits of these children may be fairly subtle, however, such that no difficulty in the child's speaking ability or listening comprehension may be readily apparent.

If in the hearing population even subtle phonological deficits are associated with poor reading, then how is it possible for profoundly deaf individuals to read? One might suppose that deaf persons would have difficulty with reading, and, indeed, this is the case. Surveys have consistently shown that hearing impaired students lag significantly behind their normally hearing counterparts in reading achievement (Conrad 1979; Furth 1966; Trybus and Karchmer 1977). Although it is typical to state, based on these surveys, that the average hearing impaired student graduating from high school reads only at about the level of a hearing child of fifth grade, that statistic obscures the even greater reading deficiency of *profoundly* hearing impaired students, that is, those who could be considered truly deaf. For them, the statistics are even more discouraging: Profoundly deaf students graduating from high school read, on the average, only at the level of a normally hearing child of third grade (Conrad 1979; Karchmer, Milone and Wolk 1979). Remember, though, that these reading achievement scores represent only a population average. We find, for example, that measures of reading achievement for deaf students attending Gallaudet University may average seventh to tenth grade, with some students reading at above the twelfth grade level (see, for example, Hanson 1988; Hanson and Feldman 1989; Hanson, Shankweiler and Fischer 1983; Reynolds 1975).

These statistics on reading achievement levels of deaf students have been used by investigators to argue two opposing views of the relationship between phonology and reading. The assumption common to both views is that the hearing impairment of these students prevents access to English phonology. In one view, access to phonological information is believed to be crucial for reading and the generally low reading achievement levels of deaf students are believed to reflect its importance. Because these readers presumably lack access to English phonology, their acquisition of reading suffers as a consequence. The second view takes the position that access to phonological information is not important in reading. The fact that *some* deaf individuals are able to attain fairly high reading levels is taken as evidence of this. Again, the assumption is that these readers, due to their hearing impairment, lack access to phonological information. Consequently, if they succeed at reading it must be without benefit of phonology.

Neither of these positions need to be correct, however, in their interpretation of the reading achievement of deaf students. Deaf readers, despite their hearing impairment, might have access to phonology that could be used to support skilled reading. To assume that deaf readers lack access to phonology because of their deafness confuses a sensory deficit with a cognitive one. While the term *phonological* is often used to mean acoustic/auditory, or sound, this usage reflects a common misunderstanding of the term. Phonological units of a language are not sounds, but rather a set of meaningless primitives out of which meaningful units are formed. These primitives are related to gestures articulated by the vocal tract of the speaker (see Liberman and Mattingly 1985 for a more detailed discussion).[1] In the case of English, the deaf individual could learn about the phonology of the language from the motor events involved in speech production, through experience in lipreading, or from experience with the orthography.

As a rule, deaf children in English-speaking countries receive intensive instruction in speaking and lipreading. This is true both in schools that use an oral education approach (with speech being the only means of communication used in the classroom) and in schools that use a simultaneous or total communication approach (with speech being accompanied by manual communication in the classroom). Through this speech training, prelingually, profoundly deaf individuals develop varying skill in speaking and lipreading. Although some of these individuals develop quite good speaking and lipreading skills, most do not (Conrad 1979; Smith 1975). Speech training, nevertheless, does provide the deaf individual with a means of learning English phonology.

Speech intelligibility does not necessarily indicate, however, the extent to which a deaf reader has access to phonological information. Intelligibility reflects the degree to which a deaf speaker's speech can be understood by a listener. Among the things that can affect intelligibility are phonation and prosodic information. While such features clearly add to intelligibility, they may not be relevant for an individual's internal manipulation of phonological information. In any event, it cannot simply be assumed that deafness necessarily blocks access to English phonology. This is a question for empirical investigation.

How do congenitally, profoundly deaf readers who read well

manage to do it? That is the question to be addressed here. It is possible that deaf readers read English as if it were a logographic language; namely, treating printed English words as visual characters, without taking into account the correspondences between the printed letters and the phonological structure of words. Research on the reading of Japanese and Chinese, however, has suggested that for logographic languages, as for alphabetic languages, phonetic recoding of words is one component of a linguistic processing system required for the task of reading (Erickson, Mattingly, and Turvey 1977; Mann 1985; Tzeng, Hung, and Wang 1977). For example, Tzeng et al. (1977) found that the phonetic composition of printed Chinese characters influenced sentence processing for skilled readers of Chinese. These investigators concluded that even in cases where lexical access is possible without phonological mediation, a phonetic code is still required for effective processing in working memory.

The deaf individuals who participated in the studies to be discussed here had backgrounds in which sign was used predominantly. That is, they generally *had* or *were* receiving instruction using sign language. Most of these individuals considered American Sign Language (ASL), to be their preferred means of communication. ASL is the common form of communication used by members of deaf communities across the United States and parts of Canada. It is a visual-gestural language that has developed independently from spoken languages and from other signed languages. For many of the subjects in the studies reported here, ASL was their first language, having been learned as a native language from deaf parents. These subjects were typically undergraduates at Gallaudet University. All were profoundly deaf. These deaf subjects, therefore, can be characterized as having higher than average reading levels and not being exposed to an exclusively oral background.

Findings on Phonetic Coding in Working Memory

Evidence reviewed elsewhere in this monograph indicates that hearing children who are poor readers have a language deficit that is specific to the phonological domain. For example, in tests of short-term memory hearing poor readers recall fewer items overall and display less sensitivity to rhyme than hearing good readers (see, for example, Shankweiler et al. 1979). That is, on rhyming lists, the accuracy of the good readers is typically worse than on nonrhyming lists. In contrast, the accuracy of the poor readers is about the same for rhyming and nonrhyming lists. The good readers' differential performance on recall of rhyming and nonrhyming strings has been taken to mean that these readers convert the printed letters into a phonetic form and retain this phonetic information in memory. Accordingly, the finding that poor readers are not much affected by rhyming manipulations suggests that they are less able to use the phonetic information.

Is a phonetic code uniquely well-suited to the task of reading? To examine this question, we asked whether for deaf signers a different language code, one based on the structure of signs, could provide an alternative coding system for reading.

A sign of ASL is produced by a combination of the formational parameters of handshape, place of articulation, movement, and orientation (Battison 1978; Stokoe, Casterline, and Croneberg 1965). Evidence indicates that when *signs* are presented for recall in a short-term memory task, the signs are coded in terms of these formational parameters. The first line of evidence comes from studies on intrusion errors in the recall of lists of signs (Bellugi, Klima, and Siple 1975; Krakow and Hanson 1985). In the study by Bellugi, Klima, and Siple, lists of spoken words or signs were presented to hearing adults and deaf adults, respectively. The subjects were asked for immediate written recall. Intrusion errors for the hearing group were confusions of phonetically similar words. For example, a subject might write the word *boat* instead of the word presented, "vote." Errors for the deaf subjects, however, were completely different; they were confusions of the formational parameters of signs. As an example, a subject might write the word *egg* instead of the sign presented, NAME. The signs corresponding to the words *name* and *egg* differ only in terms of the movement of the hands (see fig. 1).

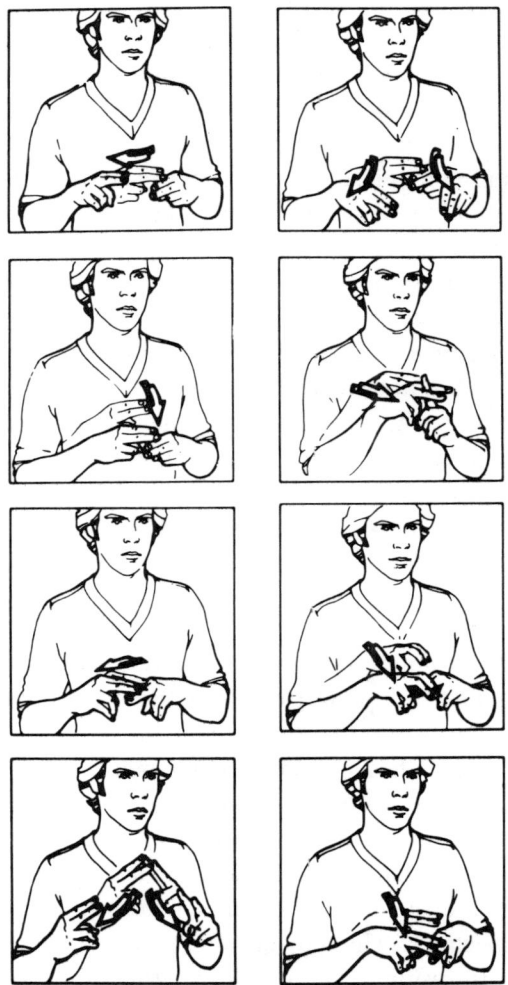

Fig. 1. Formationally similar signs. Shown left to right from the top are KNIFE, EGG, NAME, PLUG, TRAIN, CHAIR, TENT, SALT. (From Hanson 1982, 574.)

Phonology and Reading

In addition, there is evidence that lists of formationally similar signs can produce performance decrements in serial recall tasks (Hanson 1982; Poizner, Bellugi, and Tweney 1981). For example, shown in figure 1 is a set of formationally similar signs that I used in one such study (Hanson 1982). Shown here are, left to right from the top, the signs for KNIFE, EGG, NAME, PLUG, TRAIN, CHAIR, TENT, and SALT. On each trial in that experiment, deaf college students were shown five of the signs from this set and were asked to remember the five signs in order. Results of that experiment indicated that fewer signs were recalled from lists made up of signs from this formationally similar set than from lists made up of signs from a formationally unrelated (control) set.

Despite such evidence that sign coding can thus mediate short-term recall of *signs,* evidence from other research does not support the notion that a sign code can serve as a viable code in the service of skilled adult reading. In another condition of that study (Hanson 1982), I tested deaf college students in a short-term recall task of *printed* words. There were three types of word lists of interest here: rhyming words, orthographically similar words, and words whose signs were formationally similar. The words in the rhyming set were *two, blue, who, chew, shoe, through, jew,* and *you.* The words in the orthographically similar set were visually similar. The words in this set were *bear, meat, head, year, learn, peace, break,* and *dream.* While argument could be taken with the degree of visual similarity of the words in this list, it is at least true that these words are more similar visually than were the words in the rhyming list. The words in this visually similar set served as a control to ensure that any potential rhyme effects could not be attributed to the visual similarity of the printed words. The words in the formationally similar set were words whose corresponding signs were formationally similar. These were the words *knife, name, plug, train, chair, tent,* and *salt,* whose corresponding signs are shown in figure 1. Each of these sets was paired with a control set of words. Of interest in this experiment were any differences in ability to recall an experimental and control set.

The pattern of results in the experiment clearly indicates the use of phonetic coding by the deaf subjects. Whereas these subjects recalled 65.4 percent of the lists in the control condition, they recalled only 47.6 percent of the lists in the phonetically similar (rhyming) condition. There was, however, no decrement on the visually similar lists, indicating that the decrement on the rhyming lists was due to phonetic, not visual, similarity.

Interestingly, I found no evidence that the deaf college students I tested were using sign coding. Their performance on lists of words having formationally similar signs and on the control lists was comparable (52.9 percent of the control lists recalled vs. 51.4 percent of the formationally similar lists recalled). Converging evidence from later research supports this finding that the better deaf readers do not use sign coding in their recall or reading of printed English words (Lichtenstein 1985; Treiman and Hirsh-Pasek 1983). More than 100 years ago, Burnet (1854) argued that sign coding would be a ponderous strategy for the deaf readers, and, thus, limited in its use to the poorer readers. By finding that the better deaf readers do not use sign coding when processing printed English words, current research on the cognitive processing of deaf readers is consistent with Burnet's speculations.

The finding that the better readers were using phonetic coding is reminiscent of the results reported by Conrad (1979) in a very large-scale study of deaf and hearing impaired students in England and Wales. Conrad tested these students in a short-term memory task of rhyming and nonrhyming lists of printed letters. Comparing their performance on this memory task with measured reading ability, Conrad found that the better readers in his deaf population recalled fewer rhyming than nonrhyming lists. Thus, the better readers were using phonetic coding.

My study with deaf signers (Hanson 1982) took Conrad's findings one step further. Conrad's subjects were from schools that generally subscribed to an oral philosophy of education. As a result, phonetic coding was the only language form available to the subjects. In my study, the deaf subjects had sign language readily available to them. In fact, all of my deaf subjects had deaf parents and reported ASL to be their first language. Yet, these signers, as skilled deaf readers, used phonetic coding in that memory task, indicating the importance of phonetic coding in short-term retention of printed material.

Sensitivity to the Phonological Structure of English Words

Additional evidence that deaf readers can access phonological information about English words is provided by studies of individual word reading. For example, one experimental paradigm that has been shown to produce phonological effects with hearing readers uses a lexical decision task in which two letter strings are shown to the subjects on every trial, one string above the other (Meyer, Schvaneveldt, and Ruddy 1974). The subjects must decide whether or not *both* of the letter strings on a trial are real English words.

In a series of three experiments, we used this paradigm with deaf college students (Hanson and Fowler 1987). There were two types of word pairs of particular interest. As shown in table 1, the first was pairs in which the two words rhymed. These rhyming words were spelled alike except for the first letter. The second type of word pair of interest was pairs in which the two

TABLE 1. Rhyming and nonrhyming pairs and their matched controls

Rhyming Pairs	Nonrhyming Pairs
save-wave	*have-cave*
fast-past	*last-east*
Rhyming Controls	Nonrhyming Controls
save-past	*have-east*
fast-wave	*last-cave*

Source of data: From Hanson and Fowler 1987, Experiment 2.

words were spelled alike except for the first letter, but the pairs did *not* rhyme. It is apparent that the rhyming and nonrhyming pairs were equally similar orthographically, differing only in the phonological similarity of the two members of a pair. We tested whether there was any difference in the response times to the rhyming and nonrhyming pairs. Since, however, response times to words vary with word familiarity and orthographic regularity, it was not possible in this study to simply compare the responses to the rhyming and nonrhyming pairs. To eliminate familiarity and regularity as confounding factors, two control conditions were used. Word pairs in the control conditions used the same words as in the rhyming and nonrhyming pairs, but were repairings of these words. Thus, the control pairs for the rhyme condition were the same words as in the rhyme condition, just paired now with different words. For example, in the rhyme condition, the words *save-wave* and *fast-past* were paired together, while in the rhyme control *save-past* were paired together and *fast-wave* were paired together. Similarly, the control pairs for the nonrhyme condition were the same words as in the nonrhyme condition, just paired with different words. By comparing each word in the rhyme and nonrhyme condition with itself in a control condition, any effects of word frequency and regularity were eliminated.

The predictions for this experiment are shown in table 2. If readers in this task did not access phonological information, then there should have been no effect due to the phonological relationships between words in a pair. That is, if the readers were using solely orthographic information, then the first equation shown here would hold; namely, that the difference be-

TABLE 2. Predictions in the Hanson and Fowler 1987 Study

If ORTHOGRAPHIC CODING, then:
Control − Rhyming = Control − Nonrhyming

If PHONOLOGICAL CODING, then:
Control − Rhyming ≠ Control − Nonrhyming

tween response times to rhyming pairs and the rhyme controls would equal the difference between response times to nonrhyming pairs and their controls. Thus, response times would be the same whether or not the words of a pair rhymed.

If, however, readers *were* accessing phonological information, then there *would* be a difference in response times as a function of phonological relationships between words in a pair. Access to phonological information would be indicated if the second equation held; namely, that the two differences in response times would not be equal. In that event, the response times would be affected by the rhyming manipulation.

For the deaf college students we tested, there *was* an effect of the phonological relationship between the words in a pair. Shown in table 3 are the response times from one experiment of that study (Experiment 2). Response times were faster for the rhyming pairs than for the matched controls. In contrast, response times were slower on the nonrhyming pairs than on the matched controls. Since the rhyming and nonrhyming pairs were equally similar orthographically, this significant difference in response times for the rhyming and nonrhyming pairs was not due to orthographic influences. As a consequence, the difference in response times to the rhyming and nonrhyming pairs could be unambiguously attributed to the discrepant phonological structures. Thus, these good deaf readers, like hearing readers, accessed phonological information when reading the words.

Most impressive is the finding that the deaf subjects in that study were not only accessing phonological information, but were doing so in a highly speeded task. It might be supposed that deaf readers would be able to access phonological information only in situations in which they have time to laboriously

TABLE 3. The Response Time (RT) Difference for the Rhyming and Nonrhyming Pairs and Their Matched Controls for Deaf College Students

Control − Rhyming (52 msec) ≠ Control − Nonrhyming (-15 msec)

Source of data: From Hanson and Fowler 1987, Experiment 2.

recover learned pronunciations. In this research, however, we found that they accessed phonological information quite rapidly, suggesting that accessing such information is a fundamental property of reading for these skilled readers.

In more recent work, we have found other evidence that skilled deaf readers are sensitive to the phonological stucture of words. For example, deaf college students, when asked to think of words that rhyme with a specific target word have been found to be able to do so (Hanson and McGarr 1989). In addition, we have found that deaf college students are able to apply principles of grapheme-phoneme correspondence in generating the correct pronunciation of letter strings not previously encountered—a skill underlying the acquisition of new words. In this latter task (Hanson 1989), I tested these students on their reading of orthographically possible nonwords; that is, pseudowords. The critical test was between pseudowords such as *flaim* that were homophonous with an actual English word (*flame*) and control pseudowords. These controls were orthographically matched pseudowords that were not homophonous with an actual English word (e.g., *proom*). Examples of stimuli from the task are shown in table 4.

In two experiments using different lists of pseudowords, a paper and pencil task tested whether subjects could identify which of several pseudowords were homophonous with English words. The actual instructions to subjects were that they were to indicate whether or not each of the "nonsense words" was

TABLE 4. Examples of Pseudohomophones and Control Pseudowords

English Word	Pseudohomophone	Control
flame	flaim	proom
dog	daug	grine
spoon	spune	fosh
tall	taul	brate
home	hoam	spail
blue	bloc	nole
noon	nune	fune

Source: Selection of stimulus items from Hanson 1989, based on Mcdonald 1988.

pronounced like a real English word. In both experiments, deaf college students were able to correctly make this judgment with better than chance accuracy, although they were not as accurate as the hearing subjects. As an additional aspect of this pseudohomophone task, subjects in one of the two experiments were asked to indicate *which* English word they thought a pseudoword was pronounced like, if they had indicated that they thought it was pronounced like one. In this second task, deaf subjects were usually able to supply the correct English word.

Studies on individual word reading thus indicate that it is possible for deaf readers to have access to English phonology. This does not mean that such access is easy for these readers. Nor does it mean that all or even most deaf readers are able to use this information. The point, rather, is that hearing loss alone does not preclude access to phonology. In addition, it is important to note that the better deaf readers generally take advantage of this phonological information.

Why Phonological Coding?

In sum, the evidence, which has been summarized here, indicates that it is possible for deaf readers to use phonology. The use of phonological information tends to be characteristic of deaf good readers, whether they are beginning readers (Hanson, Liberman, and Shankweiler 1984), high school students (Conrad, 1979; McDermott 1984), or college students (Hanson 1982; Hanson and Fowler 1987; Lichtenstein 1985). Why would the better deaf readers use this type of linguistic information when reading? One possibility has to do with the structural properties of particular languages. In English, where word order is relatively fixed, grammatical structuring is essentially sequential. A phonological code may be an efficient medium for retaining the sequential information that is represented in English.

Deaf individuals have specific difficulty in the recall of temporally sequential information (Hanson 1988). Studies have consistently found that the measured memory span of deaf individuals is shorter than that of hearing persons (see, for example, Bellugi, Klima, and Siple 1975; Blair 1957; Belmont and Karchmer 1978; Conrad 1979; Hanson 1982; Kyle 1980; Pintner and Paterson 1917; Wallace and Corballis 1973). It is important to note that this finding of a short span applies not only to the English materials (e.g., lists of words, letters, or digits), but also applies to studies that have measured serial recall of *signs*. Fairly typical results were found in the Bellugi, Klima, and Siple (1975) study, in which deaf adults' correct serial recall of signs reached an asymptote with a list length of four signs, while the hearing subjects reached asymptote with lists of six words. Thus, the differences in memory span found in deaf individuals appear to be due not simply to unfamiliarity with the English material; rather, they appear to be related to cognitive processes involved in short-term memory for linguistic materials, in general.

Ability to maintain a sequence of words in short-term memory is related to the use of phonological coding. That is, studies with orally trained subjects (Conrad 1979), native signers of ASL (Hanson 1982), and subjects mixed in terms of their educational and linguistic backgrounds (Lichtenstein 1985), have all found strong correlations between the magnitude of the rhyme effect for deaf subjects and measured memory span. In these studies, the larger the rhyme effect for a deaf subject, the larger that subject's memory span. In contrast, no correlation between use of manual coding and measured memory span has been established (Lichtenstein 1985).

Given this relationship between serial recall ability and phonological coding, we have suggested that one reason the skilled deaf reader uses phonological coding may have to do with the critical syntactic role played by sequential structuring in English (Hanson 1982; Lake 1980; Lichtenstien 1985). This analysis suggests that an issue to be faced by teachers is how to educate deaf students to process a highly temporally structured language such as English.

Deaf Readers and Phonology

It is notable that the subjects in the studies discussed were not generally from oral backgrounds. In some cases, subjects were expressly selected because they were *native signers of ASL*. Yet, even these subjects, if skilled readers, were found to be using phonological information in the reading of English, rather than referring to ASL.

A discussion of phonological sensitivity in deaf readers always leads to the question of how this sensitivity is acquired. It is likely that congenitally, profoundly deaf readers acquire phonology from a combination of three sources: experience with the orthography through reading, experience in speaking, and experience in lipreading. In many of the studies discussed here, there was evidence of phonological processing for deaf subjects whose speech was not intelligible. That even these subjects use phonological coding suggests that deaf individuals' ability to use phonological information when reading is not well reflected in the intelligibility ratings of their speech. Further research is needed to determine the type of language instruction capable of promoting access to the speech skills most relevant to reading.

When this chapter was first planned, it was titled "Is reading different for deaf individuals?" The answer appears to be both yes and no. Clearly the answer is yes in the sense that deaf readers will bring to the task of reading very different sets of language experiences than the hearing child. These differences will require special instruction. But, the answer is also no. The evidence indicates that skilled deaf readers use their knowledge of the structure of English when reading. Although sign coding, in theory, might be used as an alternative to phonological coding for deaf signers, the research using various short-term memory and reading tasks has found little evidence that words are processed with reference to sign by the better deaf readers. Rather, the better deaf readers, like the better hearing readers, have learned to abstract phonological information from the orthography, despite congenital and profound hearing impairment.

The finding of phonological processing by deaf readers, particularly deaf readers skilled in ASL, makes a strong case for the importance of phonological sensitivity in the acquisition of skilled reading, whether the reader is hearing or deaf. For deaf readers, the acquisition and use of phonological information is extremely difficult. They would be expected to use alternatives such as visual (orthographic) or sign strategy, if such were effective. Yet, the evidence indicates that the successful deaf readers do not rely on these alternatives.

NOTES

This writing of this chapter was supported, in part, by Grant NS-18010 from the National Institute of Neurological and Communicative Disorders and Stroke. I wish to thank Carol Padden for her thoughtful reading of an earlier version of this manuscript.

1. The term *phonology* need not be limited to use with spoken language. In the case of American Sign Language, for example, the term phonology has been used to describe the linguistic primitives related to the visible gestures by the hands, face, and body of the signer. In the present chapter, however, phonology will be restricted in reference only to features related to spoken languages.

REFERENCES

Battison, R. 1978. *Lexical Borrowing in American Sign Language.* Silver Spring, Md.: Linstok Press.

Bellugi, U.; Klima, E. S.; and Siple, P. 1975. Remembering in signs. *Cognition* 3:93–125.

Belmont, J. M., and Karchmer, M. A. 1978. Deaf people's memory: There are problems testing special populations. In *Practical Aspects of Memory,* ed. M. Gruneberg and R. Sykes. London: Academic Press.

Blair, F. X. 1957. A study of the visual memory of deaf and hearing children. *American Annals of the Deaf* 102:254–63.

Burnet, J. R. 1854. The necessity of methodical signs considered. *American Annals of the Deaf* 7:1–14.

Conrad, R. 1979. *The Deaf Schoolchild.* London: Harper and Row.

Erickson, D.; Mattingly, I. G.; and Turvey, M. T. 1977. Phonetic activ-

ity in reading: An experiment with Kanji. *Language and Speech* 20:384–403.
Furth, H. G. 1966. A comparison of reading test norms of deaf and hearing children. *American Annals of the Deaf* 111:461–62.
Hanson, V. L. 1982. Short-term recall by deaf signers of American Sign Language: Implications for order recall. *Journal of Experimental Psychology: Learning, Memory, and Cognition* 8:572–83.
———. 1988. Recall of order information by deaf signers: Clues to memory span deficits. Manuscript.
———. 1989. On the use of grapheme-phoneme correspondences by deaf readers. Manuscript.
Hanson, V. L., and Feldman, L. B. 1989. Language specificity in lexical organization: Evidence from deaf signers' lexical organization of ASL and English. *Memory and Cognition* 17:292–301.
Hanson, V. L., and Fowler, C. A. 1987. Phonological coding in word reading: Evidence from hearing and deaf readers. *Memory and Cognition* 15:199–207.
Hanson, V. L.; Liberman, I. Y.; and Shankweiler, D. 1984. Linguistic coding by deaf children in relation to beginning reading success. *Journal of Experimental Child Psychology* 37:378–93.
Hanson, V. L., and McGarr, N. S. 1989. Rhyme generation by deaf adults. *Journal of Speech and Hearing Research* 32:2–11.
Hanson, V. L.; Shankweiler, D.; and Fischer, F. W. 1983. Determinants of spelling ability in deaf and hearing adults: Access to linguistic structure. *Cognition* 14:323–44.
Karchmer, M. A.; Milone, M. N., Jr.; and Wolk, S. 1979. Educational significance of hearing loss at three levels of severity. *American Annals of the Deaf* 124:97–109.
Krakow, R. A., and Hanson, V. L. 1985. Deaf signers and serial recall in the visual modality: Memory for signs, fingerspelling, and print. *Memory and Cognition* 13:265–72.
Kyle, J. G. 1980. Sign coding in short term memory in the deaf. In *Proceedings of the First International Symposium on Sign Language Research,* ed. B. Bergman and I. Ahlgren. Stockholm: Swedish National Association of the Deaf.
Lake, D. 1980. Syntax and sequential memory in hearing impaired children. In *Proceedings of the Gallaudet Conference on Reading in Relation to Deafness,* ed. H. N. Reynolds and C. M. Williams. Washington, D.C.: Division of Research, Gallaudet College.
Liberman, A. M., and Mattingly, I. G. 1985. The motor theory of speech perception revised. *Cognition* 21:1–36.
Liberman, I. Y. 1971. Basic research in speech and lateralization of

language: Some implications for reading disability. *Bulletin of the Orton Society* 21:71–87.

———. 1973. Segmentation of the spoken word and reading acquisition. *Bulletin of the Orton Society* 23:65–77.

Lichtenstein, E. H. 1985. Deaf working memory processes and English language skills. In *Cognition, Education, and Deafness: Directions for Research and Instruction,* ed. D. S. Martin. Washington, D.C.: Gallaudet College Press.

McDermott, M. J. 1984. The role of linguistic processing in the silent reading act: Recoding strategies in good and poor deaf readers. Ph.D. diss., Brown University.

Macdonald, C. J. M. 1988. Can oral-deaf readers use spelling-sound information to decode? Manuscript.

Mann, V. A. 1985. A cross-linguistic perspective on the relation between temporary memory skills and early reading ability. *Remedial and Special Education* 6:37–42.

Meyer, D. E.; Schvaneveldt, R. W.; and Ruddy, M. G. 1974. Functions of graphemic and phonemic codes in visual word-recognition. *Memory and Cognition* 2:309–21.

Pintner, R., and Paterson, D. G. 1917. A comparison of deaf and hearing children in visual memory for digits. *Journal of Experimental Psychology* 2:76–88.

Poizner, H.; Bellugi, U.; and Tweney, R. D. 1981. Processing of formational, semantic, and iconic information in American Sign Language. *Journal of Experimental Psychology: Human Perception and Performance* 7:1146–59.

Reynolds, H. N. 1975. Development of reading ability in relation to deafness. *World Congress of the World Federation of the Deaf: Full Citizenship for All Deaf People.* Washington, D.C.: National Association for the Deaf.

Shankweiler, D.; Liberman, I. Y.; Mark, L. S.; Fowler, C. A.; and Fischer, F. W. 1979. The speech code and learning to read. *Journal of Experimental Psychology: Human Learning and Memory* 5: 531–45.

Smith, C. R. 1975. Residual hearing and speech production in deaf children. *Journal of Speech and Hearing Research* 18:795–811.

Stokoe, W. C., Jr.; Casterline, D.; and Croneberg, C. 1965. *A Dictionary of American Sign Language.* Washington, D.C.: Gallaudet College Press.

Treiman, R., and Hirsh-Pasek, K. 1983. Silent reading: Insights from congenitally deaf readers. *Cognitive Psychology* 15:39–65.

Trybus, R., and Karchmer, M. 1977. School achievement scores of hearing impaired children: National data on achievement status and growth patterns. *American Annals of the Deaf* 122:62–69.

Tzeng, O. J. L.; Hung, D. L.; and Wang, W. S-Y. 1977. Speech recoding in reading Chinese characters. *Journal of Experimental Psychology: Human Learning and Memory* 3:621–30.

Wallace, G., and Corballis, M. C. 1973. Short-term memory and coding strategies in the deaf. *Journal of Experimental Psychology* 99: 334–48.

CHAPTER 4
The Role of Language-Related Factors in Reading Disability

William E. Tunmer

Abstract

Several views regarding the role of language-related factors in reading disability are examined. It is suggested that poor metalinguistic ability may be the subtle language deficiency that is primarily responsible for the difficulties experienced by many children in learning to read. A two-year longitudinal study was conducted to determine more precisely the relation of metalinguistic abilities to beginning reading. One hundred first grade children were administered a test of verbal intelligence, a test of decentration ability, two tests of metalinguistic ability (phonological awareness and syntactic awareness), a test of listening comprehension, and three tests of reading achievement. These tests were readministered to the children in second grade. Results suggested that listening comprehension and phonological recoding are the proximal causes of individual differences in reading ability, that phonological and syntactic awareness are essential for acquiring phonological recoding skill, that syntactic awareness also makes an independent contribution to listening comprehension performance, and that deficient metalinguistic ability is the result of a developmental lag in decentration ability.

Résumé

Plusieurs points de vue sur le rôle des facteurs liés au langage dans les incapacités de lecture sont examinés. Il est suggéré qu'une mauvaise compétence métalinguistique pourrait être une déficience de langage subtile qui est principalement responsable des difficultés qu'ont beaucoup d'enfants à apprendre à lire. Une étude longitudinale a été menée pendant deux ans pour déterminer plus précisément le rapport de la compétence métalinguistique avec le commencement de l'apprentissage de la lecture. On a fait subir à cent enfants dans leur première année de scolarité un test d'intelligence verbale, un test de compétence de décentration, deux tests de compétence métalinguistique (conscience phonologique et conscience syntactique), un test de compréhension orale et trois tests de lecture. On a refait ces tests en deuxième année. Les résultats semblent indiquer que la compréhension orale et le recodage phonologique sont les causes proximales des différences individuelles en ce qui concerne l'aptitude à la lecture, que la conscience syntactique et la conscience phonologique sont essentielles pour l'acquisition du mécanisme de recodage phonologique, que la conscience syntactique aussi contribue indépendamment à la comprehension orale, et qu'une mauvaise compétence métalinguistique est le résultat d'un retard du développement en compétence de décentration.

Zusammenfassung

Es werden verschiedene Gesichtspunkte bezüglich der Rolle der sprachbezogenen Faktoren der Leseunfähigkeit untersucht. Es wird deutlich gemacht, dass Defizite in den metalinguistischen Fähigkeiten für die feinen Sprachunzulänglichkeiten verantwortlich sein dürften, die den Kindern beim Erlernen einer Sprache die Hauptschwierigkeiten bereiten.

Eine Studie, die sich über den Zeitraum von zwei Jahren erstreckte, wurde durchgeführt, um die Relation von metalinguistischen Fähigkeiten zu Beginn des Lesens präziser zu bestimmen. Einhundert Erstklässler wurden mit einem Test auf dezentrierende Fähigkeit, einem Test auf verbale Intelligenz, zwei Tests auf metalinguistische Fähigkeit (phonologisches Bewusstsein und syntaktisches Bewusstsein), einem Test auf Gehörverständnis und drei Tests auf Leseaufführung untersucht. Diese Tests wurden bei den Kindern in der zweiten Klasse wiederholt.

Die Ergebnisse zeigten, dass Gehörverständnis und phonologische Aufnahmefähigkeit die nächstliegenden Gründe der individuellen Unterschiede bezüglich der Leseunfähigkeit sind, dass phonologisches und syntaktisches Bewusstsein wesentlich sind, Fähigkeiten in phonologischer Aufnahmefähigkeit zu erlangen, dass syntaktisches Bewusstsein ebenfalls einen unabhängigen Beitrag zum Gehörverständnis liefert und dass unzureichende metalinguistische Fähigkeit das Resultat einer Entwicklungsverzögerung der Dezentrationsfähigkeiten ist.

Resumen

Este trabajo investiga la influencia ejercida sobre la capacidad de lectura por parte de algunos factores relacionados con el lenguaje. La hipótesis fundamental es que las dificultades que muchos niños experimentan en la lectura son debidas principalmente a una deficiencia lingüística sutil, a saber, una escasa capacidad metalingüística. Se llevó a cabo un estudio longitudinal de dos años para determinar con mayor precisión la relación de la capacidad metalingüística con el inicio de la lectura. Cien niños de primer año de enseñanza primaria fueron sometidos a un test de inteligencia verbal, un test de capacidad de decentración, dos tests de capacidad metalingüística (consciencia fonológica y consciencia sintáctica), un test de comprensión auditiva, y tres tests de nivel de actuación en la lectura. Otros tres tests fueron pasados a niños de segundo año de enseñanza primaria. Los resultados sugieren que la comprensión auditiva y la recodificación fonológica son las causas inmediatas de las diferencias individuales en la capacidad de lectura, que las consciencias fonológica y sintáctica son esenciales para lograr una recodificación fonológica satisfactoria, que la consciencia sintáctica también interviene en el proceso de comprensión auditiva, y que una capacidad metalingüística deficiente es debida a un retraso en el desarrollo de la capacidad de decentración.

Recent theories of reading disability in children have tended to reject nonverbal deficit theories in favor of explanations that focus on deficiencies in language and linguistic coding. Vellutino and Scanlon (1982), for example, review the theoretical arguments and empirical evidence in support of theories of reading disability that assume deficits in visual processing, cross-modal transfer, serial memory, attention, association learning, or rule learning and conclude that all these theories are untenable. They propose instead that specific reading disability is due primarily to deficits in verbal processing.

With respect to the latter, however, there are many possibilities. First, since the reading process is grafted onto the listening process, it is almost axiomatic that children who lack proficiency in the language being read will encounter reading difficulties. Accordingly, deficiencies in the different levels of language functioning would be expected to result in different kinds of reading difficulty (Menyuk and Flood 1981). Children who have problems in perceiving speech should have difficulty in learning to decode words. That is, children who are unable to discriminate between different types of phonemes, perhaps because of a high frequency hearing loss, should encounter difficulty in analyzing speech and relating it to print. Children with poorly developed lexical representations should have difficulty in comprehending words after they have been recognized. Children who are deficient in syntactic knowledge should have difficulty in understanding sentential relations in written sentences. And children who have problems in integrating the propositions underlying sentences into larger sets of interrelated propositions through the application of pragmatic and inferential rules should have difficulty in comprehending and recalling stories and passages.

It is little wonder then that children who suffer impairments in one or more of the various domains of language are much more likely to encounter reading problems than children with normal oral language skills (Mann 1986). With respect to specific reading disability, however, this observation is of little interest because the children under consideration are, by definition, "not ostensibly impaired in language and suffer no grossly debilitating disorders in this function" (Vellutino and Scanlon 1982, 191). If some aspect of language processing is causally related to reading disability, it must be of a more subtle nature.

Decontextualized language use is one possibility. Preschool speech is highly concrete and bound to the specific situation. As Donaldson (1978) describes it, child language during this period is, for the most part, "embedded . . . in the flow of events that accompany it" (88). In contrast, the language of text is a more context independent, elaborated form of code. Idea units in written language are larger and more syntactically complex than they are in spoken language (Chafe 1985). Such linguistic devices as nominalization, subordination, and modification are used to pack many idea units into a single sentence. In addition, cohesion, the process of linking together the sentences of running discourse, is lexicalized in written language; the sentences of text are tied together by cohesive elements. In contrast, spoken discourse cohesion is accomplished primarily through situational context and paralinguistic and prosodic cues. Beginning readers who are unfamiliar with decontextualized language use may therefore encounter difficulties in learning to read.

Wells (1985) has suggested that listening to stories during the preschool years may facilitate the development of decontextualized language use. In support of this suggestion, Wells found that of three preschool activities—drawing, looking at picture books, and listening to stories—the latter was significantly related to later reading comprehension performance. A major difficulty with this study, however, is that story listening was also significantly related to the level of educational attainment of the children's parents, which is known to be correlated with children's general intelligence. Since Wells did not administer an intelligence test to the children, it is possible that general verbal ability was responsible for the observed relationship between story listening and reading comprehension.

General verbal ability is another possible candidate for the subtle language deficiency that causes reading problems in some children. Research has shown that poor readers tend to perform less well on tests of verbal intelligence than on tests of nonverbal intelligence, and that performance differences between good and poor readers are greater on the Verbal Subscales of the Wechsler Intelligence Scale for Children (WISC) than on the performance subscales (see Vellutino 1979 for a review). The question that arises, however, is whether the relatively low verbal IQ of the poor readers is a cause or consequence of reading difficulty. Normal readers read more than poor readers and are therefore exposed to more verbal material, a possible consequence of which is the development and practice of the normal readers' general verbal abilities.

Data relevant to this issue comes from a four-year longitudinal study conducted by Bishop and Butterworth (1980). An initial sample of 189 four-year-old children was administered the Wechsler Pre-school and Primary Scale of Intelligence (WPPSI). Four years later 139 of these children were administered the WISC and the Neale Analysis of Reading Ability. The results indicated that the data obtained from the children when they were eight years of age replicated the findings of earlier studies. Performance on the verbal subtests of the WISC was more closely related to reading achievement than was performance on the nonverbal subtests, and the poor readers performed less well on the verbal subtests than on the nonverbal subtests. However, examination of the four year olds' scores revealed that the verbal and nonverbal scores were equally related to later reading achievement, and that children who subsequently became poor readers were not at the time particularly weak in the verbal subtests of the WPPSI. These findings suggest that general verbal deficits observed among disabled readers are probably a consequence of reading failure rather than a cause of it.

Deficiency in using language prediction skills to identify words is another language-related explanation of reading problems. According to this view, fluent reading is primarily an activity of using the syntactic and semantic redundancies of language to generate hypotheses or guesses about the text yet to be encountered (Goodman 1967; Smith 1971). Efficient readers are thought to pay little attention to the bulk of the words of text because the flow of language follows a predictable pattern. Instead, they use the fewest cues possible to make a prediction and test their guess against their developing meaning. Unlike fluent readers, poor and beginning readers are less able to make use of contextual redundancy, according to this position.

A major assumption of this conceptualization of reading is that learning to read is a natural process not unlike the acquisition of spoken language. Reading failure is thought to result from methods of reading instruction that conflict with the natural course of events. Word study activities should therefore emphasize the process of "making meaning," not the mechanics of reading words in isolation or translating written words into sounds, because the latter would prevent the reader from making important generalizations through context cues.

Research conducted during the past fifteen years has not supported this explanation of reading failure. Several studies have shown that contrary to what would have been expected from the claims of Goodman and Smith, the effect of context on reading performance *decreases* with increasing age, grade level, reading ability, word familiarity, and stimulus quality (see Stanovich 1986 for a review). On the basis of these findings, Stanovich (1980) concluded that less skilled readers compensate for difficulties in word recognition by relying more on sentence context to facilitate ongoing word recognition. The superior word recognition ability of better readers appears to make reliance on contextual information to generate hypotheses about the upcoming words of text largely unnecessary.

Even more damaging to the views of Goodman and Smith is the finding that context will enable the *skilled* reader, under ideal conditions, to predict no more than one word in four (Gough 1983). Moreover, the words that can be predicted correctly are typically frequently occurring function words rather than less frequently occurring but more meaningful context words. These findings suggest that for beginning readers heavy reliance on context to identify unfamiliar words will result in little progress, as the words that beginning readers can correctly predict from context will tend to be the words that they can already recognize (Gough and Hillinger 1980). Consistent with this suggestion is research by Biemiller (1970) who found in a longitudinal study of first graders' oral reading errors that older and better readers relied more on decoding than contextual guessing, and that progress in reading was determined in part by how early children shifted their attention to graphic information.

In opposition to the views of Goodman and Smith is Perfetti's (1985, 1986) verbal efficiency theory. This theory maintains that reading problems are primarily due to two interrelated factors: inefficient word recognition and deficient phonetic short-term memory. A central claim of verbal efficiency theory is that inefficient lexical access disrupts the temporary representation of text in working memory. As words are recognized, their phonological representations are stored in working memory until sufficient information has accumulated to permit assembly of the lexical entries into larger units of relational meaning called propositions. Since proposition encoding takes place within the limits of working memory, lexical access that is inefficient and capacity draining would disrupt the temporary representation of text in working memory, and comprehension would suffer as a result. Evidence in support of this claim comes from studies reporting strong correlations between speed of word recognition and reading comprehension, especially among children in the lower grades (see Perfetti 1985). That the relationship between word recognition speed and reading comprehension is a causal one is supported by a longitudinal study by Lesgold, Resnick, and Hammond (1985). Using a cross-lag panel design, Lesgold and colleagues obtained a pattern of correlations that suggested word recognition speed in first grade was causally related to reading comprehension in the second and third grades.

Verbal efficiency theory also assumes that reading problems are the reflection of a deficiency in the ability to maintain and operate on verbal material in working memory (Perfetti 1986). This suggests that disabled readers may suffer from a "double handicap" (Liberman and Shankweiler 1985; Shankweiler and Crain 1986). Not only are they unable to use their phonetic short-term memory efficiently because of slow word recognition, but their short-term memory capacity appears to be unusually constrained as well. Liberman and Shankweiler (1985) hypothesize that both aspects of this double handicap are linked to an underlying deficit in phonological processing.

Evidence in support of the claim that the short-term memory ability of disabled readers is unusually constrained comes from studies showing that poor readers perform less well than normal readers on tasks requiring the ordered recall of strings of digits, letters, nameable objects, nonsense syllables, or words. These deficiencies appear to be limited to the language domain, since other kinds of materials, such as nonsense designs and faces, can generally be retained in working memory without deficit by poor readers (for reviews see Liberman and Shankweiler 1985; Mann 1986; Shankweiler and Crain 1986).

The general conclusion drawn from these studies, however, has been questioned by Bryant (1986). He points out that the evidence cited in support of the verbal working memory deficit hypothesis is based on studies comparing good and poor readers of similar age and intelligence. The problem with this type of research design, argues Bryant, is that it yields uninterpretable results when a difference in some reading-related variable is found (for an opposing view, see Shankweiler et al., forthcoming). The difference could be either a cause or a consequence of reading failure.

Good readers differ from poor readers in the amount of practice they receive in reading. This additional reading experience may improve the efficiency of verbal working memory in at least two ways. First, as noted earlier, it has been found that idea units in written language are significantly longer and more syntactically complex than those of spoken language (Chafe 1985). Since better readers are exposed to more written language than poor readers, they receive more practice in maintaining complex linguistic structures in working memory, a possible consequence of which is an improvement in their ability to make effective use of phonological representations in working memory. Second, it is possible that repeated practice with grapheme-phoneme correspondences improves children's ability to maintain a phonological code in memory (Tunmer, forthcoming). That is, improved efficiency in verbal working memory could be a spin-off effect of the metalinguistic operations (see the next section) that children must perform to become skilled readers. Differences in verbal working memory ability may therefore be a consequence of differences in reading ability rather than a cause of them.

Another possibility is that verbal working memory ability is both a cause and a consequence of learning to read; that is, there may be a reciprocal relation between efficient verbal working memory and reading achievement. Differences in verbal working memory ability may cause differences in the ease with which children learn to read. However, the process of learning to read itself may directly influence the development of verbal working memory ability. Further research is required to test this hypothesis.

Metalinguistic Abilities and Reading Disability

The central claim of this chapter is that poor metalinguistic ability is the subtle language deficiency that is most closely related to problems in learning to read. Metalinguistic ability enables one to reflect on and manipulate the structural features of spoken language. It is a developmentally distinct kind of linguistic functioning that develops separately from and later than basic speaking and listening skills. The ability to treat language as an object of thought is not an automatic consequence of language acquisition. In support of this claim are the results of studies that show that many five- and six-year-old children who appear to possess normal language processing skills are unable to perform such simple metalinguistic operations as counting the number of phonemes in spoken words or correcting word order violations in simple sentence structures (see Tunmer, Pratt, and Herriman 1984 for reviews of research on the development of metalinguistic abilities in children).

Unlike normal language operations, which involve automatic processing, metalinguistic operations require control processing. Language users do not normally notice such things as the individual phonemes and words comprising an utterance, the grouping relationships among its constituent words, or whether the utterance is structurally ambiguous or synonymous with another utterance, unless they deliberately think about it; that is, unless they invoke control processing to reflect on the structural features of the utterance. Here the phrase "structural features" refers to the intuitive notion that words are built up from phonemes, sentences are built up from words, and sets of interrelated propositions are built up from the propositions underlying individual sentences.

The relationship between normal language processing and metalinguistic operations can be expressed in terms of a model of sentence comprehension that specifies a set of interacting processors in which the output of each becomes the input to the next (Tunmer, forthcoming; Tunmer and Herriman 1984). According to the model, a speech perception mechanism, by means not fully understood, converts the acoustic signal into a sequence of phonemes. The phonemes then serve as the input to a lexical access mechanism that (somehow) groups the phonemes and searches a mental lexicon to find the meanings of the words in the utterance. Another processor, sometimes referred to as a parser, takes the words retrieved from the lexicon and builds a structural representation of them, from which the utterance's meaning is derived. Individual propositions, however, do not normally stand in isolation but are integrated into larger sets of propositions through the application of pragmatic and inferential rules.

The model provides the basis for a definition of metalinguistic awareness as the ability to use control processing to perform mental operations on the products of the mental mechanisms involved in sentence comprehension (i.e., the phonemes, words, sentences, and sets of interrelated propositions). The model also provides the basis for classifying the various manifestations of metalinguistic awareness into four broad categories: phonological, word, syntactic, and pragmatic awareness. Phonological and word awareness refer to the ability to reflect on and manipulate the subunits of spoken language, the phonemes and words. Syntactic awareness refers to the ability to perform mental operations on the output of the mechanism responsible for assigning intrasentential structural representations to groups of words. And pragmatic awareness refers to the ability to perform mental operations on the output of the mechanism responsible for integrating individual propositions into larger sets of propositions through the application of pragmatic and inferential rules. Examples of phonological awareness include segmentation of words and pseudowords into their constituent phonemes, recognition of rhyme, blending of phonemic units, phoneme deletion, phoneme substitution, and appreciation of puns. Examples of word awareness include segmentation of sentences or phrases into words, separation of words from their referents, appreciation of jokes involving lexical ambiguity, judgment of word length, recognition of synonyms and antonyms, and word substitution. Examples of syntactic awareness include detection of structural ambiguity in sentences, recognition of synonymy relations, correction of word order violations, and completion of sentences with missing words. And examples of pragmatic awareness include detection of inconsistencies between sentences, recognition of message inadequacy, understanding of communication failures, and awareness of macrostructures.

Of the four general types of metalinguistic ability, phonological awareness has attracted the greatest attention. On logical grounds alone it would appear that at least some minimal level of explicit phonological awareness is required to discover the systematic correspondences between graphemes and phonemes, the knowledge of which would enable beginning readers to identify words not seen before and to gain the levels of practice necessary for developing speed and automaticity in recognizing words (Gough and Hillinger 1980; Jorm and Share 1983; Stanovich 1986). In support of these claims are studies showing that letter-sound knowledge is intimately related to the acquisition of basic reading skills (Backman et al. 1984; Manis and Morrison 1985), that training in phonemic segmentation skill produces significant experimental group advantages in reading achievement (Bradley and Bryant 1983; Olofsson and Lundberg 1985), and that phonological awareness influences reading comprehension indirectly through phonological recoding ability, the ability to apply the grapheme-phoneme correspondence rules (Stanovich, Cunningham, and Feeman 1984; Tunmer and Nesdale 1985). Evidence that some minimal level of explicit phonological awareness is necessary for being able to learn to read comes from a study that we conducted in which a scatterplot was presented displaying the relationship between phonemic segmentation ability and pseudoword decoding, a measure of phonological recoding (Tunmer and Nesdale 1985). The scatterplot showed that although there were many children who performed well on phoneme segmentation but poorly on pseudoword decoding, there were no children who performed poorly on phoneme segmentation but well on pseudoword decoding (see also Juel, Griffith, and Gough 1986; Tunmer, Herriman, and Nesdale 1988).

Although word awareness also develops during middle childhood (Ehri 1975; Tunmer, Bowey, and Grieve 1983) and appears to be related to beginning reading achievement (Bowey, Tunmer, and Pratt 1984; Evans, Taylor, and Blum 1979; McNich 1974) there is no need to treat it separately from phonological awareness, because phonological awareness implies word awareness. That is, the ability to reflect on phonemes presupposes an awareness that the connection between a spoken word and its referent is an arbitrary one, that the sound used to represent a concept is not an inherent property of the concept. For example, to segment the spoken word *dog* into its constituent phonemic elements, children must first be able to dissociate the sound "dog" from the concept to which it refers. They can then analyze the sound into its phonemic elements.

More recently, researchers have begun to examine the role of syntactic awareness in learning to read. Several studies using a variety of different tasks (e.g., judgment of grammaticality, correction of word order violations or morpheme deletions, oral cloze) have demonstrated that syntactic awareness is related to beginning reading achievement (see Ryan and Ledger 1984 for a review). The evidence linking syntactic awareness and reading ability, however, is correlational, typically involving designs in which reading disabled subjects are matched in age with normal readers. The problem with such designs is that the normal readers will have received greater exposure to written language than their chronological age matches. As noted earlier, a possible consequence of greater reading experience is the development and practice of normal readers' verbal abilities.

To avoid the problem of interpretation resulting from differential exposure to print, Tunmer, Nesdale, and Wright (1987) used a reading-level match design in which good, younger readers were matched with poor, older readers in reading ability and verbal intelligence. The results indicated that the good readers scored significantly better than the poor readers on two measures of syntactic awareness, suggesting the possibility of a causal connection between syntactic awareness and learning to read. Two ways in which syntactic awareness may influence reading development were proposed. One way is by enabling readers to monitor their ongoing comprehension processes more effectively (Bowey 1986). Comprehension monitoring is an executive function that skilled readers use to make sense of incoming textual information (Wagoner 1983). It has been described as the process of keeping track of whether comprehension is proceeding smoothly and taking remedial action if necessary (Baker and Brown 1984).

Many poor readers appear to encounter difficulty in following the content and structure of the passage they are reading. When a breakdown in comprehension occurs, these children either fail to detect it, or if they do detect it, they are unable to employ the "fix-up" strategies necessary to improve their understanding of text. A strategy that syntactically aware children are able to use is to check that the meanings they assign to the words of spoken or written discourse conform to the surrounding grammatical context. They are also able to make intelligent guesses about the meaning of difficult words in prose passages.

The second way syntactic awareness may influence reading development is by helping children acquire word recognition skill. Researchers have generally not considered this possibility. For example, both Bowey (1986) and Willows and Ryan (1986) found that measures of syntactic awareness correlated more strongly with context-free decoding than with reading comprehension, but neither offered as an explanation of their results the possibility that syntactic awareness directly facilitates the acquisition of decoding skill.

There are three reasons for seriously considering the latter possibility. First, because the acquisition of knowledge of grapheme-phoneme correspondences is a process that takes place over time, beginning readers will not be able to recode all of the unfamiliar words that they encounter. Syntactic awareness may facilitate the development of phonological recoding skill by enabling children to combine knowledge of the constraints of sentential context with incomplete phonological information to identify unfamiliar words. As more words are correctly identified, children's knowledge of the letter-sound correspondences would increase. This contextual facilitation may be especially important for learning more complex rules, such as those whose application depends on either the position of the letter in the word or on the presence of a "marker" letter.

Second, the ability to use context may help beginning readers to discover that some spelling patterns (called *homographic* spelling patterns) are associated with more than one pronunciation. The letter sequence *ough,* for example, is pronounced differently in the words *cough, rough* and *dough.* When confronted with an unfamiliar word containing a homographic spelling pattern, beginning readers who possess such knowledge can generate alternative pronunciations until one matches a word in their listening vocabulary. Children who have yet to acquire this knowledge and are poor at using sentence-context cues to discover polyphonic letter sequences may be restricted to pronouncing *flown* like *clown,* or *clear* like *bear,* and receive misleading learning trials as a result.

Third, several investigators have argued that the ability to use context may help beginning readers learn to recognize genuine exception words, such as *pint* and *yacht* (Gough and Hillinger 1980; Jorm and Share 1983). Because no word is spelled completely arbitrarily, even exception words provide some accurate phonological cues to the word's identity (Gough and Hillinger 1980). When beginning readers apply their knowledge of letter-sound correspondences to such words, the result will often be close enough to the correct form that sentence-context cues can be used to arrive at a correct identification.

It is important to distinguish this type of contextual facilitation from that associated with the views of Goodman (1967) and Smith (1971). Goodman and Smith argue that the *automatic* use of context to predict words is the major feature of *ongoing* sentence processing, whereas the view proposed here is that the ability to deliberately reflect on sentence structures (i.e., syntactic awareness) *in combination with* emerging phonological recoding skills is essential for *acquiring* decoding skills.

Consistent with the hypothesis that syntactic awareness plays an important role in learning to decode are findings from the longitudinal study by Biemiller (1970) referred to earlier. He found that the most advanced stage of beginning reading was one in which the readers made use of *both* graphic and contextual information in word identification.

The fourth kind of metalinguistic skill, pragmatic awareness, may influence reading development by enabling readers to monitor their comprehension of text at the intersentence level. Good readers, for example, are better able to detect between-sentence inconsistencies in written text than are poor readers (e.g., Garner 1980). Unlike syntactic awareness, however, there seems to be little theoretical justification for supposing that pragmatic awareness facilitates the acquisition of phonological recoding skills. This suggests that pragmatic awareness may not be particularly important in the early stages of learning to read, when the focus is primarily on the acquisition of decoding skill, but may become more important at later stages, when the emphasis shifts more toward text-level processes (see Tunmer, Herriman, and Nesdale 1988, for evidence in support of this claim).

It is important to note that the claim that metalinguistic abilities are causally related to learning to read is not inconsistent with the possibility that the process of learning to read itself may facilitate the development of metalinguistic abilities. Some skills that are acquired or enhanced as a result of learning to read, such as the abilities to form and maintain a phonetic code in working memory and to generate orthographic images, may greatly improve performance on metalinguistic tasks. This suggests that metalinguistic ability may be both a cause and a consequence of learning to read, a phenomenon referred to as reciprocal causation. According to this view of metalinguistic development, beginning readers must achieve some minimal level of metalinguistic ability to acquire basic reading skills that, in turn, enable them to acquire the spin-off skills of reading that provide the basis for more advanced metalinguistic performances.

This interpretation of metalinguistic development may explain why adults who are not literate in an alphabetic orthography perform so poorly on tests of phonological awareness. The processing demands of the tests typically given to adult subjects are much greater than those of a simple segmentation or rhyming task. Consider, for example, the phoneme reversal task (e.g., say *pat* backward), which has been used as a measure of phonological awareness in adult illiterates (Byrne and Ledez 1983). This task requires the subject not only to segment a word into its constituent phonemic elements but also to delete the initial (or final) phoneme, move this phoneme to the end (or beginning) of the sequence of phonemes, repeat the two preceding operations a second time, and then put the segments back together again to pronounce the word. The processing demands of this task are clearly much greater than those of a simple segmentation task, since five additional operations are required. These additional operations may place such a great strain on phonetic memory that the task can be performed successfully only if subjects are able to reduce the load on their phonetic memory by generating orthographic images of the words presented to them. Most adult skilled readers probably respond to the phoneme reversal task by generating an orthographic image of the word, mentally reordering the word's letters, and then reading the result in their mind's eye. Each of these operations requires literacy skills, skills the adult illiterate does not possess.

Bryne and Ledez (1983) found that adult illiterates performed very poorly on the phoneme reversal task in comparison to normal adult readers, and interpreted this result as supporting the claim that phonological awareness is largely a consequence of literacy acquisition. However, another possibility is that the phoneme reversal task and others like it, such as the phoneme deletion task, require high levels of ability in using a phonetic code in working memory and in generating orthographic images, in which case the poor performance of the adult illiterates would be expected, since both of these skills develop with increasing reading ability. Consistent with this suggestion,

Byrne and Ledez found that in addition to being the only subjects who performed well on the phoneme reversal task, the normal adult readers were also the only subjects who were susceptible to phonological confusability (an index of the use of phonemic-coding processes in working memory) in a continuous word recognition task that included words that rhymed with target words. This finding suggests that high levels of phonemic-coding processes in working memory may be required to perform the phoneme reversal task.

Origins of Deficient Metalinguistic Abilities

Relatively little is known about the origins of deficiencies in metalinguistic abilities. Some researchers have argued that deficits in metalinguistic ability are largely dissociated from more general cognitive skills (Stanovich 1986). This conclusion may have been based in part on the finding that in the early stages of reading development, measures of general verbal ability (typically the Peabody Picture Vocabulary Test [PPVT]) are only weakly correlated with measures of metalinguistic ability or not at all. An alternative possibility, however, is that metalinguistic ability is more closely related to measures of general ability that require metacognitive operations. These are usually nonverbal and problem-solving measures of general ability as opposed to a measure like the PPVT, which is simply a measure of recognition vocabulary knowledge.

It has been suggested, for example, that metalinguistic ability may be linked to the Piagetian process of decentration (Lundberg 1978; Tunmer, forthcoming; Tunmer, Herriman, and Nesdale 1988). Metalinguistic performances such as separating a word from its referent, dissociating the meaning of a sentence from its form, and reflecting on the phonemic elements of words require the ability to decenter, to shift one's attention from message content to the properties of language used to convey content. An essential feature of both metalinguistic abilities and decentration is the ability to control the course of one's thought;

that is, to invoke control processing. According to this view, then, deficient metalinguistic ability is a reflection of a developmental lag in decentration processes.

This is not to suggest that high levels of metalinguistic ability emerge spontaneously in development. Rather, this view proposes that during middle childhood children develop the capacity for *becoming* metalinguistically aware when confronted with certain kinds of tasks, such as learning to read. Children may need first to reach a certain threshold level of decentration ability before they can perform the low-level metalinguistic operations necessary to acquire basic reading skills that, in turn, enable them to acquire the spin-off skills of reading that provide the basis for more advanced metalinguistic performances. This suggests that it is possible for children with little or no metalinguistic ability at school entry to learn to read normally provided that they possess the level of cognitive ability necessary for acquiring the requisite metalinguistic skills.

A major advantage of the decentration lag hypothesis is that it provides an explanation of why specific training in metalinguistic awareness is particularly effective for some children (see, for example, Williams 1980) but unnecessary for most others who acquire basic reading skills without such training. The decentration lag hypothesis proposes that by the time children begin formal schooling most will have developed the capacity for performing metalinguistic operations even though they may never have encountered situations that required them to do so. However, as a result of naturally occurring differences in the rate of decentration development, the control processing abilities of some children may be such that they require, or at least would greatly benefit from, explicit training in metalinguistic awareness.

In support of the decentration lag hypothesis are the results of a longitudinal study we conducted which showed that decentration ability (as measured by Piagetian tasks of concrete operativity) in preliterate children was most strongly correlated with overall metalinguistic ability at the beginning and end of first grade than was any other school-entry variable (Tunmer, Herriman, and Nesdale 1988). The latter included measures of general verbal ability, letter-name knowledge, and print awareness. In contrast, general verbal ability (as measured by the PPVT) failed to make an independent contribution to any of the metalinguistic measures either at school entry or at the end of first grade. The results further showed that preliterate children with low levels of phonological awareness at school entry but above average levels of decentration ability showed significantly greater improvement in phonological awareness during the school year than similar children with below average levels of decentration ability at school entry. The mean phonological awareness score of the high-decentration ability group was above the mean of all children's phonological awareness scores at the end of the year, whereas the low-decentration ability group mean was one standard deviation below the overall mean. This finding suggests that many preliterate children with low levels of metalinguistic ability at school entry but high levels of decentration ability should do reasonably well in learning to read even though their preliterate level of metalinguistic awareness might suggest otherwise.

A Longitudinal Study of Metalinguistic Abilities and Beginning Reading

A two-year longitudinal study was conducted to determine more precisely the roles of phonological and syntactic awareness in the beginning stages of learning to read. Toward the end of first grade, 100 children (54 boys and 46 girls with a mean age of 6 years, 2 months) were individually administered a test of phonological awareness, a test of syntactic awareness, the PPVT, a test of decentration ability (as measured by Piagetian tasks of concrete operativity), and four subtests of the Interactive Reading Assessment System (IRAS) developed by Calfee and Calfee (1981): real word decoding, pseudoword decoding, listening comprehension and reading comprehension. At the end of second grade, these tests were readministered to 84 students from the original sample.

Several hypotheses were tested in the study. First, it was predicted that pseudoword decoding (a measure of phonological recoding ability) and listening comprehension would be the strongest predictors of reading comprehension performance. Gough and Tunmer (1986) have proposed that phonological recoding and listening comprehension are the *proximal* causes of individual differences in reading comprehension. Each skill is assumed to be necessary, but not sufficient, for success in reading: the effect of either skill on reading ability depends on the reader's level of competence in the other skill. Thus, if decoding ability is high but listening comprehension skill is low, the child will be a poor reader. Conversely, if listening comprehension skill is high but decoding ability is low, the child will again be a poor reader.

The assumption that deficits in phonological recoding and listening comprehension are the proximal causes of reading failure raises the question of what gives rise to deficits in these skills. It was predicted that a path analysis would show that both phonological and syntactic awareness influence reading comprehension indirectly through phonological recoding skill, and that scatterplots of the relationships between phonological and syntactic awareness and phonological recoding would indicate that both metalinguistic abilities are necessary but not sufficient for learning the grapheme-phoneme correspondences. From the assumption that syntactic awareness also influences the development of the comprehension monitoring subcomponent of listening comprehension, it was further predicted that the path analysis would show that syntactic awareness influences reading comprehension indirectly through listening comprehension.

A final set of predictions concerned the influence of decentration ability (as measured by Piagetian tasks) and verbal intelligence (as estimated by the PPVT) on the development of metalinguistic skills. It was predicted that the concrete operativity measure would be a better predictor of metalinguistic development than the PPVT, even though the PPVT would appear to be more directly concerned with language development. Concrete operational thought and metalinguistic ability are more similar than they appear since as noted earlier, both require higher-level metacognitive operations such as decentration and control processing.

Tests and Procedures Used in the Study

The children were tested individually in a quiet room at their school. The PPVT, concrete operativity test, two metalinguistic tests, and the real word decoding and pseudoword decoding subtests of IRAS were administered in separate sessions, whereas the listening comprehension and reading comprehension subtests of IRAS were administered in a single session. All tests were administered at the end of both first and second grade during the fourth term of a four-term school year.

Form M of the PPVT (Dunn and Dunn 1981) was used to provide an estimate of each child's verbal intelligence. Standard scoring procedures were used.

A test developed by Arlin (1981) was used to measure each child's level of concrete operational thought. A total of ten tasks was presented to each child. These were: simple and double seriation; simple classification, two-way and three-way matrix classification; number conservation, conservation of continuous quantity, and conservation of discontinuous quantity; and a class inclusion task that was given twice, with two different sets of materials. The materials and procedures used in presenting these tasks were the same as those used by Arlin (1981). However, a different system of scoring was developed which gave equal weighting (6 points) to each of the four general types of tasks (seriation, class inclusion, classification, and conservation) (see Tunmer, Herriman, and Nesdale 1988). A total score of 24 points was possible on the operativity test.

A modified version of a test we had developed previously (Tunmer, Herriman, and Nesdale 1988; Tunmer and Nesdale

1982, 1985) was used to measure phonological awareness. The results of our earlier work suggested that phonemic segmentation tasks that include high-frequency real words, or else either real or synthetic words containing digraphs (letter pairs representing single phonemes, such as *sh, th, oa, ou*), may provide inaccurate estimates of phonological awareness. The set of test items was therefore made up entirely of nondigraph, nonword syllables (e.g., *zif, ud, lind*). There were twenty-two test items: five single-phoneme sounds (the short vowels), five two-phoneme syllables consisting of three VC (vowel-consonant) syllables and two CV syllables, five CVC syllables, five four-phoneme syllables (three CVCC syllables and two CCVC syllables), and two five-phoneme syllables (one CCCVC syllable and one CCVCC syllable). The test was presented in the form of a tapping game that was originally developed by Liberman et al. (1974). The children were asked to tap out the number of phonemes in each syllable spoken by the experimenter (see Tunmer, Herriman, and Nesdale 1988 for procedural details). Scoring was based on the number of items tapped correctly.

Children's syntactic awareness was assessed by an oral correction task similar to one used in earlier studies (Pratt, Tunmer, and Bowey 1984; Tunmer, Herriman, and Nesdale 1988; Tunmer, Nesdale, and Wright 1987). The children were asked to correct ungrammatical sentences from three to five words in length that contained word-order violations. This task was used instead of an oral cloze task because sentence anagram tasks are thought to require an even greater attention to form than sentence completion tasks (Ryan and Ledger 1984). Twenty-five test items were presented to each child. Twelve items were produced by rearranging the major sentence constituents: subject (S), verb (V), and object (O). There were four items for each of three types of constituent order changes: VOS, VSO, and SOV. For example, the item *made biscuits Mum* was produced by a VOS reordering of constituents. Eight items were produced by introducing one of two types of word-order change within one of the major constituents. These were reversal of article and noun and reversal of auxiliary and verb (e.g., *dog the barked, Frank painting was*). There were four items for each type of word-order change within constituents. The remaining five items were produced by completely reversing the word order of simple sentences (e.g., *hands his washed Ross*). Items were scored as correct only if the child's response was a correct reordering of the words that were presented.

Reading achievement and listening comprehension ability were assessed by four subtests of IRAS (Calfee and Calfee 1981). These were tests of real word decoding, pseudoword decoding, listening comprehension, and reading comprehension.

The real word decoding test assessed the children's ability to recognize real words. The materials consisted of eight six-word lists; the lists were in order of increasing difficulty based on word frequency, number of syllables, and complexity of letter-sound correspondence. The children were presented with the lists of words and asked to read them aloud. Reading continued until more than half the words of a given list were read incorrectly. Each item was assigned a numeric value from 0 to 3, depending on the quality of the response. A value of 0 was assigned for failure to respond or for responses that were totally incorrect. A value of 1 was given for responses that were only partially correct (e.g., initial segment correct but remaining segments incorrect); a 2 for responses that were mostly correct (e.g., completely correct except for a single consonant cluster or vowel); and a 3 for items pronounced without error.

In the pseudoword decoding task, the children were presented with lists of synthetic words that were constructed to correspond to the rules of English orthography. Six lists of words were ordered by difficulty, ranging from simple consonant-vowel-consonant patterns to blends, digraphs, and vowel variations. Before being asked to read the synthetic words aloud, the children were told that the items were not real words and had no meaning, but that they could be pronounced like English words. The scoring procedure was the same as that used for the real words.

The materials for the reading and listening comprehension subtests consisted of well-formed narrative and expository passages, ordered in difficulty based on word frequency, number of words per sentence, number of sentences, and number of propositions expressed per sentence. Each story was constructed according to the principles of story grammar, and associated with each element (setting, initiating event, attempt, outcome) was a probe question. A similar procedure was used in constructing the expository passages. The children were presented with the lowest level passage and were asked to read it aloud. If they were able to read the passage within 150 seconds, they were asked to retell as much of the passage as they could. After the children finished the free-recall task, any element that was not adequately recalled was then probed with the corresponding question. If the child recalled half or more of the passage elements under either free or cued recall, the next more difficult passage was presented until the child failed to meet this criterion.

Listening comprehension was assessed with parallel narrative and expository passages, again using the free and cued recall procedures. The startingpoint for each child was one level above the highest level attempted on the reading comprehension subtest. If the child failed the recall criterion, easier passages were presented until success was achieved.

The same scoring procedure was used for both the listening and reading comprehension subtests. After scoring elements separately for free and cued recall, each element was assigned a single value ranging from 0 to 7, based on responses under both recall conditions. A critical index was then computed, with the integer portion of the index representing the level of highest success and the decimal portion the ratio of assigned points for combined elements to total possible points for that level.

Discussion of Results

Displayed in table 1 are the intercorrelations, means, and standard deviations for all variables at each grade. For the first grade measures, concrete operativity was more strongly correlated with the metalinguistic measures than was the PPVT, as anticipated. The correlation of .53 between the two metalinguistic abilities was reasonably strong despite the fact that each was measured by a different task, one being a segmentation task and the other a correction task. The component skill common to both measures is the ability to reflect on the structural features of spoken language.

The two metalinguistic measures were also significantly correlated with the two decoding measures. Syntactic awareness, however, was more strongly correlated with both reading and listening comprehension than was phonological awareness. This finding is consistent with the suggestion that in addition to playing an important role in the acquisition of decoding skills,

TABLE 1. Intercorrelations, Means, and Standard Deviations of All Variables

Variable	1	2	3	4	5	6	7	8
1. PPVT		.44	.24	.39	.20	ns	.44	.30
2. Concrete operativity	ns		.37	.53	.32	.33	.33	.30
3. Phonological awareness	ns	ns		.53	.49	.47	.31	.31
4. Syntactic awareness	ns	.21	.21		.46	.46	.56	.42
5. Real word decoding	.28	.23	.22	.38		.85	.50	.78
6. Pseudoword decoding	ns	.35	.31	.46	.79		.50	.66
7. Listening comprehension	.39	ns	ns	.31	.46	.40		.49
8. Reading comprehension	.24	ns	.23	.35	.77	.66	.54	
M (first grade)	107.7	16.1	16.8	18.2	27.9	31.4	3.90	1.05
SD (first grade)	11.7	4.7	4.3	4.9	25.0	31.3	1.86	1.53
M (second grade)	106.0	20.5	20.5	23.5	67.9	76.1	6.08	3.77
SD (second grade)	11.8	3.3	1.9	1.6	26.2	27.0	1.40	1.47
Maximum score	140.0+	24.0	22.0	25.0	144.0	126.0	9.00	8.00

Note: Intercorrelations above the diagonal are for the first grade children, and those below are for the second grade children.

syntactic awareness is also important in the development of the comprehension monitoring subcomponent of listening comprehension. As predicted, the decoding measures and listening comprehension were more strongly correlated with reading comprehension than were any of the other variables.

For the second grade measures, the pattern of correlations was similar to that obtained with the first grade measures. However, the correlations involving concrete operations and the two metalinguistic measures were generally weaker than the corresponding first grade correlations. This result most likely reflects the fact that performance on these measures was approaching ceiling levels by the end of second grade.

To test the hypothesis that phonological and syntactic awareness are each necessary but not sufficient for learning grapheme-phoneme correspondences, a scatterplot was generated between each metalinguistic measure and pseudoword decoding (all measures were taken at the end of first grade). The scatterplots, which appear in figures 1 and 2, reveal a pattern of results similar to that observed in earlier studies (Tunmer, forthcoming; Tunmer, Herriman, and Nesdale 1988; Tunmer and Nesdale 1985). There were many children who performed well on the phonological (or syntactic) awareness test, but poorly on pseudoword decoding. However, there were no children who scored well on pseudoword decoding, but poorly on the phonological (or syntactic) awareness test. These findings suggest that both metalinguistic abilities are essential for acquiring knowledge of the grapheme-phoneme correspondences. The results also indicate that the magnitude of the correlation between each metalinguistic measure and pseudoword decoding (.47 and .46 for phonological and syntactic awareness, respectively) underestimates the strength of the relationship because each relationship is nonlinear.

To investigate further the pattern of correlations among the measures taken in first grade, the data were subjected to a path analysis. Since the two decoding measures were so highly correlated ($r = .85$), only one, pseudoword decoding, was included

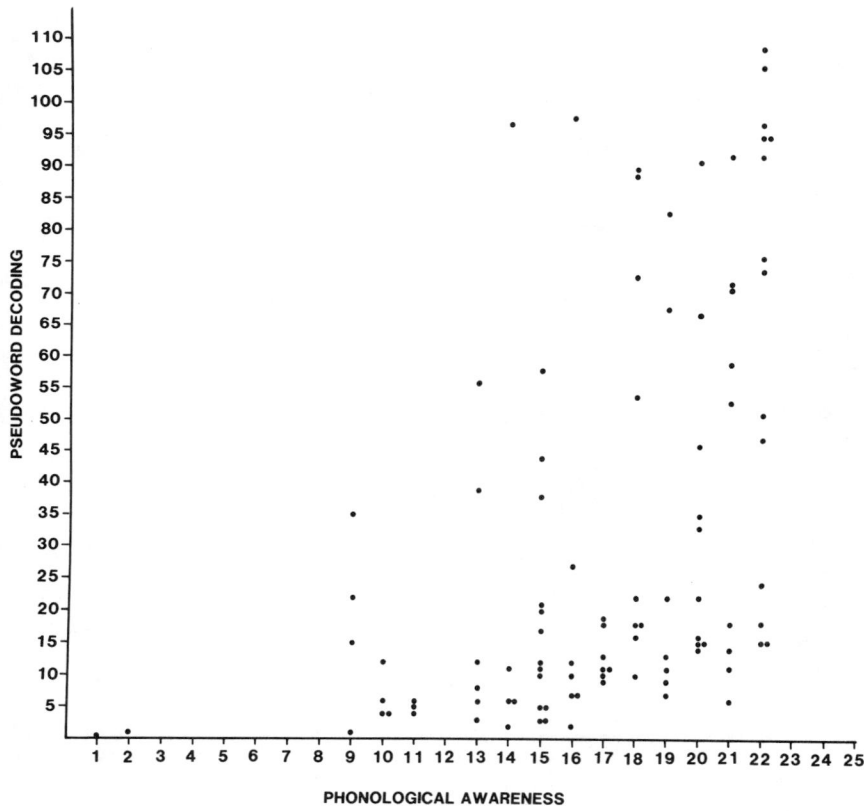

Fig. 1. Scatterplot of phonological awareness and pseudoword decoding

in the path analysis. The first step in the analysis was to determine which variables made a significant independent contribution to the variability of reading comprehension performance. Only one did, pseudoword decoding (see fig. 3). That listening comprehension did not also make a significant independent contribution to reading comprehension performance, but did do so in second grade (see below), agrees with the findings of Juel, Griffith, and Gough (1986), who obtained a similar pattern of results using different measures of decoding, listening compre-

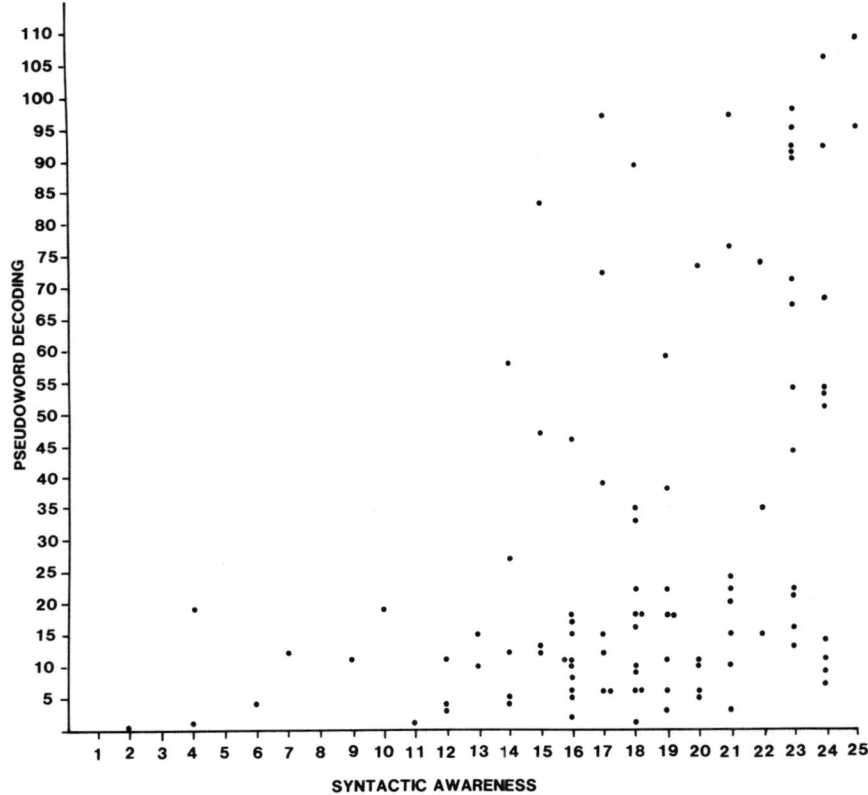

Fig. 2. Scatterplot of syntactic awareness and pseudoword decoding

hension, and reading comprehension. These results suggest that decoding skills are critical in the beginning stages of learning to read and that listening comprehension becomes more important at a somewhat later stage after children have begun to master basic decoding skills.

Of the remaining variables (verbal intelligence, concrete operativity, phonological awareness, and syntactic awareness), only the metalinguistic measures independently influenced pseudoword decoding. This finding provides support for the hypothe-

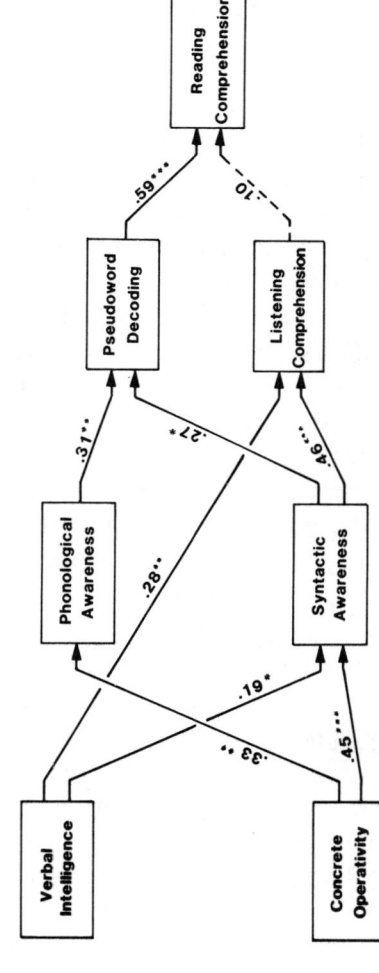

Fig. 3. Path diagram displaying structure of relationships among first grade measures. (Standardized beta weights are shown on each path; *$p < .05$, **$p < .01$, ***$p < .001$.)

sis that both phonological and syntactic awareness influence reading comprehension indirectly through phonological recoding (as measured by pseudoword decoding). Along with verbal intelligence, syntactic awareness also made an independent contribution to listening comprehension, as predicted. Phonological awareness and concrete operativity failed to make independent contributions to listening comprehension. Concrete operativity did, however, independently influence both phonological and syntactic awareness. This result is consistent with the hypothesis that decentration ability (as measured by concrete operativity) is more strongly related to metalinguistic ability than is verbal intelligence. Verbal intelligence did make an independent contribution to syntactic awareness, but the path coefficient barely reached significance. A possible explanation of this latter finding is that unlike the phonological awareness task, performance on the syntactic awareness task depends in part on vocabulary knowledge, which, in the present study, was used as an estimate of verbal intelligence. Word knowledge includes knowledge about the syntactic structures into which words can enter. Since such knowledge is required to perform a word-order correction task, children with superior vocabulary knowledge would have an advantage, all other things being equal.

The predictive correlations between the metalinguistic and general ability measures taken in first grade and the achievement measures taken in second grade are presented in table 2. Concrete operativity appears to be more strongly related to later achievement than is verbal intelligence, perhaps because of its influence on the development of metalinguistic skills, which, as can be seen in table 2, are even more strongly related to later achievement than is operativity. Although both phonological and syntactic awareness are significantly correlated with the second grade decoding measures, only syntactic awareness predicts later achievement in listening comprehension. This result is similar to what was found with the first grade measures. Syntactic awareness not only appears to influence the development of phonological recoding skill, but appears to influence the development of listening comprehension skill as well.

A second path analysis was performed to determine more precisely the structure of relationships between the first grade ability measures and the second grade achievement measures (see fig. 4). The analysis revealed that listening comprehension and pseudoword decoding were the only variables to make significant independent contributions to reading comprehension performance. This finding supports the claim that listening comprehension and phonological recoding are the proximal causes of individual differences in reading comprehension performance. The pattern of results for the remaining variables was identical to that observed in the path analysis for the first grade measures with one exception: verbal intelligence in first grade failed to independently influence second grade listening comprehension performance. Overall, the findings are impressive because they show that metalinguistic ability in first grade is significantly related to listening and reading achievement in second grade, even after the effects of verbal intelligence and concrete operativity have been removed.

With respect to reading disability, there were three children whose reading comprehension scores in second grade were

TABLE 2. Predictive Correlations between First Grade Ability Measures and Second Grade Achievement Measures

Predictor Variable	Second Grade Achievement Measures			
	Real Word Decoding	Pseudoword Decoding	Listening Comprehension	Reading Comprehension
PPVT	.25*	.12	.28**	.25*
Concrete operativity	.33***	.36***	.29**	.32***
Phonological awareness	.41***	.43***	.04	.36***
Syntactic awareness	.54***	.46***	.35***	.46***

*$p < .05$ **$p < .01$ ***$p < .001$

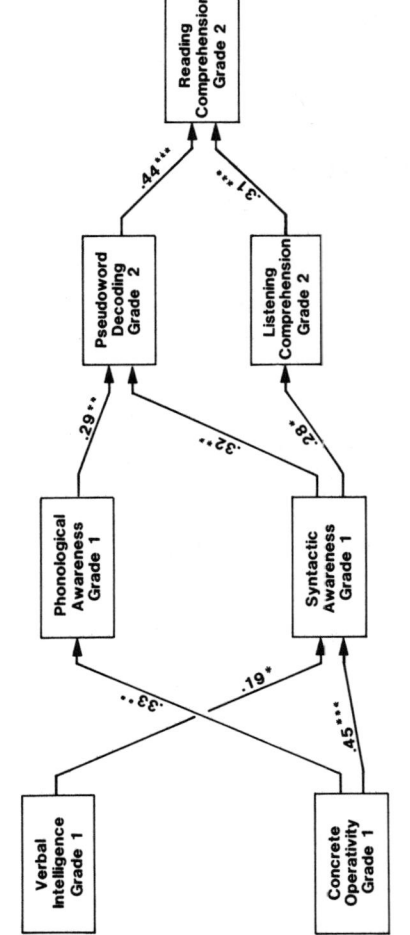

Fig. 4. Path diagram displaying structure of relationships between first grade ability measures and second grade achievement measures. (Standardized beta weights are shown on each path; *$p < .05$, **$p < .01$, ***$p < .001$.)

more than two standard deviations below the mean for all the children. Since these children's PPVT scores in second grade were in the normal range (124, 94, 118) they would be classified as reading disabled under standard criteria. Significantly, the means of these children's first grade metalinguistic scores were 9.7 for phonological awareness and 10.3 for syntactic awareness. Both means were considerably below the means for all children (see table 1), which suggests that markedly deficient metalinguistic ability in the early stages of learning to read may be the subtle language deficiency responsible for the severe reading problems encountered by some beginning readers.

Concluding Remarks

The results of our work suggest that metalinguistic ability plays a critical role in the acquisition of reading skill and that deficient metalinguistic ability in beginning readers is the result of a developmental lag in decentration ability. This lag in development may delay early progress in reading to such an extent that it initiates what Stanovich (1986) describes as a "cascade of interacting achievement failures and motivational problems" (393). Deficient metalinguistic ability is therefore seen not as evidence of a specific cognitive deficit, but rather as an indication of a slower rate of cognitive development, which can be partially overcome by intensive training in metalinguistic skills. However, such training must be initiated as early as possible to avoid the snowballing consequences of reading failure that Stanovich (1986) describes.

For example, with respect to metalinguistic development, children who are developmentally delayed in decentration processes may suffer a "double whammy." These children's level of decentration ability may be such that they cannot readily perform the low-level metalinguistic operations necessary for acquiring basic reading skills. Consequently, they will not be able to derive maximum benefit from reading instruction and will fail to acquire the spin-off skills of reading that provide the basis for developing more advanced metalinguistic skills, skills which facilitate further growth in reading. In short, the reciprocal relationship between metalinguistic development and reading achievement is blocked from the outset. As noted earlier, this interpretation of metalinguistic development would explain why adults who are not literate in an alphabetic orthography perform so poorly on tests of phonological awareness that require a high level of phonological processing in working memory.

An alternative view to the decentration lag hypothesis is that deficient metalinguistic ability is the reflection of a more general deficiency in the ability to maintain and operate on verbal material in working memory (Liberman and Shankweiler 1985; Shankweiler and Crain 1986). Delay in the development of metalinguistic ability is seen as reflecting limitations on the *use* of phonological structures in working memory (Shankweiler and Crain 1986). The results of the present study are not inconsistent with this interpretation. The two tasks used to measure phonological and syntactic awareness are, in effect, short-term memory tasks, although short-term memory tasks of a particular sort, namely, those involving the ability to reflect on the structural features of spoken language.

A possible difficulty with the verbal working memory deficit hypothesis, however, is that metalinguistic tasks themselves would appear to provide excellent measures of the operation of verbal working memory, in which case the explanation of deficient metalinguistic ability in terms of deficient verbal working memory becomes somewhat circular. Verbal working memory is generally viewed as comprising two components, a phonological store that holds unorganized linguistic information very briefly and a limited capacity central executive that is used to operate control processes. Metalinguistic operations would appear to involve both of these components. The essential question that remains is what gives rise to deficiencies in metalinguistic abilities and other skills that require phonological processing in working memory. The decentration lag hypothesis proposes that a developmental delay in the control processing component of working memory initiates a sequence of events that results in deficits in *both* reading skills and phonological processing skills.

Regardless of which hypothesis turns out to be correct, studies have shown that metalinguistic ability is causally related to reading achievement even when differences in short-term memory ability are controlled (e.g., Bradley and Bryant 1983). It is therefore possible that verbal short-term memory deficits and developmental lags in metalinguistic ability both contribute to reading failure. Further research is required to test this hypothesis.

NOTE

This research was supported by a grant from the Australian Research Grants Scheme. The author expresses appreciation to the staff and the students of Leeming Primary School (Perth, Western Australia) who participated in the research, and to Colleen Harvey and Mary Rohl who helped in data collection and analysis.

REFERENCES

Arlin, P. 1981. Piagetian tasks as predictors of reading and math readiness in grades K–1. *Journal of Educational Psychology* 73:712–21.

Backman, J.; Bruck, M.; Hebert, M.; and Seidenberg, M. S. 1984. Acquisition and use of spelling-sound correspondences in reading. *Journal of Experimental Child Psychology* 38:114–33.

Baker, L., and Brown, A. L. 1984. Metacognitive skills and reading. In *Handbook of Reading Research,* ed. P. D. Pearson, R. Barr, M. Kamil, and P. Mosenthal. New York: Longman.

Biemiller, A. 1970. The development of the use of graphic and contextual information as children learn to read. *Reading Research Quarterly* 6:75–96.

Bishop, D. V. M., and Butterworth, G. E. 1980. Verbal-performance discrepancies: Relationship to birth risk and specific reading retardation. *Cortex* 16:375–90.

Bowey, J. A. 1986. Syntactic awareness in relation to reading skill and ongoing reading comprehension monitoring. *Journal of Experimental Child Psychology* 41:282–99.

Bowey, J.; Tunmer, W.; and Pratt, C. 1984. Development of children's understanding of the metalinguistic term *word. Journal of Educational Psychology* 76:500–12.

Bradley, L., and Bryant, P. E. 1983. Categorizing sounds and learning to read—a causal connection. *Nature* 301:419–21.

Bryant, P. 1986. Phonological skills and learning to read and write. In *Acquisition of Reading Skills: Cultural Constraints and Cognitive Universals,* ed. B. R. Foorman and A. W. Siegel. Hillsdale, N.J.: Erlbaum.

Byrne, B., and Ledez, J. 1983. Phonological awareness in reading-disabled adults. *Australian Journal of Psychology* 35:185–97.

Calfee, R. C., and Calfee, K. H. 1981. Interactive reading assessment system (IRAS). Manuscript, Stanford University, California.

Chafe, W. 1985. Linguistic differences produced by differences between speaking and writing. In *Literacy, Language, and Learning: The Nature and Consequences of Reading and Writing,* ed. D. Olson, N. Torrance, and A. Hildyard. Cambridge: Cambridge University Press.

Donaldson, M. 1978. *Children's Minds.* Glasgow: Collins.

Dunn, L., and Dunn, L. 1981. *Peabody Picture Vocabulary Test.* Circle Pines, Minn.: American Guidance Service.

Ehri, L. C. 1975. Word consciousness in readers and prereaders. *Journal of Educational Psychology* 67:204–12.

Evans, M.; Taylor, N.; and Blum, I. 1979. Children's written language awareness and its relation to reading acquisition. *Journal of Reading Behaviour* 11:7–19.

Garner, R. C. 1980. Monitoring of understanding: An investigation of good and poor readers' awareness of induced miscomprehension of text. *Journal of Reading Behaviour* 12:55–63.

Goodman, K. S. 1967. Reading: A psycholinguistic guessing game. *Journal of the Reading Specialist* 6:126–35.

Gough, P. B. 1983. Context, form, and interaction. In *Eye Movements in Reading: Perceptual and Language Processes,* ed. K. Rayner. New York: Academic Press.

Gough, P. B., and Hillinger, M. L. 1980. Learning to read: An unnatural act. *Bulletin of the Orton Society* 30:179–96.

Gough, P. B., and Tunmer, W. E. 1986. Decoding, reading, and reading disability. *Remedial and Special Education* 7:6–10.

Jorm, A. F., and Share, D. L. 1983. Phonological recoding and reading acquisition. *Applied Psycholinguistics* 4:103–47.

Juel, C.; Griffith, P. L.; and Gough, P. B. 1986. Acquisition of literacy: A longitudinal study of children in first and second grade. *Journal of Educational Psychology* 78:243–55.

Lesgold, A.; Resnick, L. B.; and Hammond, K. 1985. Learning to read: A longitudinal study of word skill development in two curricula. In *Reading Research: Advances in Theory and Practice,* ed. G. E. Mackinnon and T. G. Waller. New York: Academic Press.

Liberman, I. Y., and Shankweiler, D. P. 1985. Phonology and the problems of learning to read and write. *Remedial and Special Education* 6:8–17.

Liberman, I. Y.; Shankweiler, D. P.; Fischer F. W.; and Carter, B. 1974. Explicit syllable and phoneme segmentation in the young child. *Journal of Experimental Child Psychology* 18:201–12.

Lundberg, I. 1978. Aspects of linguistic awareness related to reading. In *The Child's Conception of Language,* ed. A. Sinclair, R. J. Jarvella, and W. J. M. Levelt. Berlin: Springer-Verlag.

McNich, G. H. 1974. Awareness of aural and visual word boundary within a sample of first graders. *Perceptual and Motor Skills* 38:1127–34.

Manis, F. R., and Morrison, F. J. 1985. Reading disability: a deficit in rule learning? In *Cognitive Development in Atypical Children,* ed. L. S. Siegel and F. J. Morrison. New York: Springer-Verlag.

Mann, V. A. 1986. Why some children encounter reading problems: The contribution of difficulties with language processing and language sophistication to early reading disability. In *Psychological and Educational Perspectives on Learning Disabilities,* ed. J. K. Torgesen and B. Y. Wong. New York: Academic Press.

Menyuk, P., and Flood, J. 1981. Linguistic competence, reading, writing problems and remediation. *Bulletin of the Orton Society* 31:13–28.

Olofsson, A., and Lundberg, I. 1985. Evaluation of long term effects of phonemic awareness training in kindergarten. *Scandinavian Journal of Psychology* 26:21–34.

Perfetti, C. A. 1985. *Reading Ability.* New York: Oxford University Press.

———. 1986. Cognitive and linguistic components of reading ability. In *Acquisition of Reading Skills: Cultural Constraints and Cognitive Universals,* ed. B. R. Foorman and A. W. Siegel. Hillsdale, N.J.: Erlbaum.

Pratt, C.; Tunmer, W. E.; and Bowey, J. A. 1984. Children's capacity to correct grammatical violations in sentences. *Journal of Child Language* 11:129–41.

Ryan, E., and Ledger, G. 1984. Learning to attend to sentence structure: Links between metalinguistic development and reading. In *Language Awareness and Learning to Read,* ed. J. Downing and R. Valtin. New York: Springer-Verlag.

Shankweiler, D., and Crain, S. 1986. Language mechanisms and reading disorder: A modular approach. *Cognition* 24:139–68.

Shankweiler, D.; Crain, S.; Brady, S.; and Macaruso, P. Forthcoming. Identifying the causes of reading disability. In *Reading Acquisition,* ed. P. B. Gough. Hillsdale, N.J.: Erlbaum.

Smith, F. 1971. *Understanding Reading: A Psycholinguistic Analysis of Reading and Learning to Read.* New York: Holt, Rinehart and Winston.

Stanovich, K. 1980. Toward an interactive compensatory model of individual differences in the development of reading fluency. *Reading Research Quarterly* 16:32–71.

———. 1986. Matthew effects in reading: Some consequences of individual differences in the acquisition of literacy. *Reading Research Quarterly* 21:360–406.

Stanovich, K. E.; Cunningham, A. E.; and Feeman, D. J. 1984. Intelligence, cognitive skills, and early reading progress. *Reading Research Quarterly* 19:278–303.

Tunmer, W. E. Forthcoming. Cognitive and linguistic factors in learning to read. In *Reading Acquisition,* ed. P. B. Gough. Hillsdale, N.J.: Erlbaum.

Tunmer, W. E.; Bowey, J. A.; and Grieve, R. 1983. The development of young children's awareness of the word as a unit of spoken language. *Journal of Psycholinguistic Research* 12:567–94.

Tunmer, W. E., and Herriman, M. L. 1984. The development of metalinguistic awareness: A conceptual overview. In *Metalinguistic Awareness in Children: Theory, Research, and Implications,* ed. W. E. Tunmer, C. Pratt, and M. L. Herriman. Berlin: Springer-Verlag.

Tunmer, W. E.; Herriman, M. L.; and Nesdale, A. R. 1988. Metalinguistic abilities and beginning reading. *Reading Research Quarterly* 23:134–58.

Tunmer, W. E., and Nesdale, A. R. 1982. The effects of digraphs and pseudowords on phonemic segmentation in young children. *Applied Psycholinguistics* 3:299–311.

———. 1985. Phonemic segmentation skill and beginning reading. *Journal of Educational Psychology* 77:417–27.

Tunmer, W. E.; Nesdale, A. R.; and Wright, A. D. 1987. Syntactic awareness and reading acquisition. *British Journal of Developmental Psychology* 5:25–34.

Tunmer, W. E.; Pratt, C.; and Herriman, M. L. 1984. *Metalinguistic Awareness in Children: Theory, Research and Implications.* Berlin: Springer-Verlag.

Vellutino, F. R. 1979. *Dyslexia: Theory and Research.* Cambridge, Mass.: MIT Press.

Vellutino, F. R., and Scanlon, D. M. 1982. Verbal processes in poor and normal readers. In *Verbal Processes in Children,* ed. C. J. Brainerd and M. Pressley. New York: Springer-Verlag.

Wagoner, S. A. 1983. Comprehension monitoring: What it is and what we know about it. *Reading Research Quarterly* 18:328–46.

Wells, G. 1985. Preschool literacy-related activities and success in school. In *Literacy, Language, and Learning: The Nature and Consequences of Reading and Writing,* ed. D. R. Olson, N. Torrance, and A. Hildyard. Cambridge: Cambridge University Press.

Williams, J. P. 1980. Teaching decoding with an emphasis on phoneme analysis and phoneme blending. *Journal of Educational Psychology* 72:1–15.

Willows, D., and Ryan, E. 1986. The development of grammatical sensitivity and its relationship to early reading achievement. *Reading Research Quarterly* 21:253–66.

CHAPTER 5

Why Poor Readers Misunderstand Spoken Sentences

Stephen Crain

Abstract

To help us correctly diagnose the special problems of reading, this chapter outlines a model of the processes involved in *spoken* sentence comprehension. Drawing upon a modular conception of the language apparatus, it distinguishes several levels of structural representation and several special-purpose processing mechanisms. This view of the functional architecture of language allows us to advance specific hypotheses about the causes of impaired performance in children with reading difficulties. To permit a test among these hypotheses, a methodology is introduced for disentangling subcomponents of the language apparatus that are intertwined in ordinary language use. There follows an illustrative experiment with sentences containing adjectives with exceptional control properties, such as "easy" in "The bear is easy to reach." The results (together with additional findings discussed by Shankweiler) support the view that spoken language comprehension failures by poor readers arise from limitations in phonological processing involving working memory. This conclusion challenges the hypothesis that their reading difficulties reflect a developmental lag in the acquisition of syntax.

Résumé

Afin de nous aider à diagnostiquer correctement les problèmes particuliers à la lecture, ce chapître-ci décrit un modèle des procès compris dans la compréhension des phrases parlées. Utilisant une conception modulaire de l'appareil linguistique, le modèle distingue entre plusieurs niveaux de représentation structurelle en addition de plusieurs mécanismes de procès aux buts particuliers. Cette manière de comprendre l'architecture fonctionelle du langage nous donne la possibilité de proposer des hypothèses spécifiques vis-à-vis les causes de l'exécution endommagée chez les enfants qui ont des difficultés à lire. Afin de mettre ces hypothèses à l'épreuve, on donne une prescription méthodologique pour rendre plus clairs les sous-composants qui se sont enchevêtrés dans l'usage normal du langage. On suit cette prescription dans une expérience illustrative qui utilise des phrases comprenant des adjectifs qui ont des qualités de contrôle exceptionelles, tel que *easy* dans la phrase *The bear is easy to reach*. Les résultats (mis avec d'autres résultats qu'a discutés Shankweiler) donnent plus d'évidence à la vue que les échecs dans la compréhension du langage parlé chez les lecteurs faibles sont l'issu des limitations dans les procès phonologiques qui ont à faire avec la mémoire immédiate. Cete conclusion présente un défi à l'hypothèse que leur difficultés à lire reflètent un décalage développemental dans l'acquisition de la syntaxe.

Zusammenfassung

Dieses Kapitel beschreibt ein Modell des Verstehens gesprochener Sätze, welches erlaubt Sprachverständnisschwierigkeiten schwacher Leser zu erklären. Das Modell unterscheidet mehrere Stufen der strukturellen Analyse, sowie etliche spezialisierte Verarbeitungsmechanismen. Durch diese Annahmen wird es möglich, spezifische Hypothesen über die Ursachen der erwähnten Schwierigkeiten zu formulieren und Methoden zu entwickeln, die verschiedene Komponenten des Sprachverarbeitungssystems voneinander trennen. Als Beispiel dient ein Experiment mit Sätzen, die Adjektive mit ungewöhnlichen Funktionen enthalten (z.B., "easy" in "The bear is easy to reach"). Die Ergebnisse dieser und anderer von Shankweiler diskutierter

Studien legen nahe, dass Sprachverständnisschwierigkeiten schwacher Leser von eingeschränkter phonologischer Verarbeitung im Arbeitsgedächtnis herrühren, und nicht von einer langsameren Entwicklung der syntaktischen Kompetenz.

Resumen

Para ayudarnos a diagnosticar correctamente los problemas especiales asociados con la lectura, este capítulo esquematiza un modelo de los procesos implicados en la comprensión de oraciones habladas. Basado en una concepción modular del lenguaje, el modelo distingue entre varios niveles de representación estructural, así como entre varios mecanismos de descodificación con propósitos especiales. Esta concepción de la arquitectura funcional del lenguaje nos permite avanzar hipótesis específicas acerca de las causas de actuación deficiente por parte de niños con dificultades en la lectura. A fin de contrastar tales hipótesis, se aplica un procedimiento metodológico que permite desentramar subcomponentes del lenguaje que se encuentran entremezclados en su uso normal. Este procedimiento se utiliza en un experimento ilustrativo con frases con adjetivos que poseen propiedades excepcionales de control, como es el caso de "fácil" en la frase "el oso es fácil de alcanzar." Los resultados (junto con otros resultados comentados por Shankweiler) confirman la teoría de que los errores en la comprensión del lenguaje hablado entre lectores deficientes son debidos a limitaciones en la clase de procesamiento fonológico asociado con la memoria funcional. Esta conclusión cuestiona la hipótesis de que las dificultades en la lectura reflejan un retraso evolutivo en la adquisición de la sintaxis.

In dealing with failures in language comprehension, care must be taken to distinguish a structural deficit in linguistic knowledge from a limitation in processing that knowledge, such as might result from an impairment in working memory, syntactic parsing, or sentence planning. Research on language acquisition has made significant gains in recent years in assessing the linguistic knowledge of young children and in distinguishing it from other knowledge and abilities that affect performance. This chapter sketches out some methods that have been devised to tease apart structure and process in the study of language acquisition and suggests how these methods can be applied in the study of reading disability. Recent conceptual and empirical developments put us in a position to uncover the linguistic competence and identify the causes of impaired language performance in poor readers. The results we have obtained to date undercut the widespread assumption that children with exceptional difficulty in learning to read necessarily suffer from a lack of knowledge about the structural properties of language. As we will show, the source of their language comprehension problems may lie elsewhere.

Two Explanations of Reading Disorder

Learning to read and write depends on abilities that are language related, so it seems quite natural to suppose that poor reading is the consequence of poor language skills. In keeping with this, one viewpoint about the source of reading problems sees them as reflecting a developmental lag in the acquisition of complex linguistic structures. We have called this the *structural deficit hypothesis* (Crain and Shankweiler 1988).

The structural deficit hypothesis appears to meet both practical and theoretical needs. It provides an account of why children who are poor readers often fail to perform as well as good readers in comprehending spoken sentences. It is now well established that poor readers have difficulty with some spoken sentences. The structural deficit hypothesis explains these difficulties as a consequence of a delay in language development. It assumes that full control of some of the more complex grammatical structures is not complete at the age when most children are learning to read. Poor readers, then, are doubly handicapped on this view; they are poor at orthographic decoding and they are delayed in grammar formation.

An alternative proposal looks for a single source for both problems of the poor reader, viewing each as the consequence of a limitation in processing phonological information. We have referred to this as the *processing limitation hypothesis*. According to this hypothesis, speech processing is highly automatic by the time a child begins reading, so even long stretches of speech do not ordinarily place excessive burdens on the language processing system (see Shankweiler, in this volume, for additional evidence bearing on the two hypotheses). By contrast, learning to read is difficult for most children because, at the early stages at least, comprehension of text requires additional skills to interface an orthography with preexisting language structures and processors. Until the beginning reader has achieved a considerable level of skill, the assimilation of information into the language processing system is constrained by the reader's degree of mastery in alphabetic decoding. The poor decoding skills of the beginner create a "bottleneck" that curtails syntactic and semantic analysis of the text. That is why decoding measures are usually closely associated with measures of children's comprehension of text.

Throughout this volume, it is argued that reading disabled children have unusual difficulties in processing phonological information and that this limitation is manifested not only in reading, but also in activities involving spoken language, including understanding some spoken sentences. This is seen to be a consequence of the architecture of the language processing system, in which information is transferred bottom-up through the system, so that a limitation in phonological processing creates a constriction on the flow of information. Working memory plays a central role in the argument. Working memory is seen to control the information flow between levels of the language processing system, beginning with the transfer of phonological chunks of material upward to higher levels of processing. However, since working memory is a limited resource device, any significant disruption in information flow caused by deficient phonological analysis could limit the assimilation of information into higher-level structures.

Since poor readers are known to have a deficit in phonological processing, proponents of the processing limitation hypothesis were led to anticipate that their comprehension of spoken language would be impaired, but only in some instances. Phonological limitations would be expected to perturb spoken language comprehension only with sentence structures that impose severe memory demands. On sentences that are less taxing of this resource, poor readers would be expected to perform as well as good readers. On the structural deficit hypothesis, by contrast, since poor readers are considered to be language delayed, they are expected to make significant errors in tasks that involve comprehension of sentences having complex syntactic structures, regardless of whether these sentences impose heavy demands or light demands on processing components such as working memory.

Consideration of these alternative accounts of the comprehension problems of poor readers makes it clear that we must be cognizant of all aspects of sentence comprehension if we are to distinguish a limitation in processing from a deficit in structural knowledge. It remains to spell out in more detail what is required to disentangle these various factors in an experiment whose goal is to determine whether a syntactic deficit or a processing limitation is the cause of misunderstanding by poor readers. This is the purpose of the next section. Following this, the two competing hypotheses about the source of reading disability are put to a test.

The Modularity Hypothesis

In disentangling structure and process, it is important to keep in mind that it is performance, not competence, that is directly observed. And since performance involves a number of levels of linguistic representation, as well as a number of processors that access and operate on these representations, analytic tools are required to isolate the subcomponents of the total task of sentence understanding. The problem is compounded by the speed at which the various mechanisms operate. The flow of information through the linguistic system is so fast that even with on-line tasks we run the risk of mistakenly attributing a deficit to the wrong level of representation or processor and failing to identify the actual culprit.

Despite some outstanding problems, progress has been made both in the theory of language performance and in designing tools for disentangling structural deficits from processing limitations. Instrumental to this progress, in my view, is a proposal about the functional architecture of the brain—the modularity hypothesis. The modularity hypothesis, which can be traced back to Gall, maintains that some brain functions are organized autonomously (e.g., the language faculty and stereoscopic depth perception). Each of the "modules" is autonomous in the sense that it exploits special neural structures that are specific to it and not shared by other systems.

In the case of language, one source of evidence for the modularity hypothesis comes from studies of speech perception (Liberman and Mattingly 1985). Another source is from the study of aphasia where there is evidence that a lesion in circumscribed locations in the left cerebral hemisphere may selectively perturb language performance, leaving many other cognitive abilities relatively intact. There is also evidence that language may be preserved in the face of massive losses to other systems, as in cases of the syndrome of "isolation of the language function" (e.g., Whitaker 1976). A further source of evidence for modularity is from the study of language development, where it has been found that complex linguistic principles emerge in young children at a characteristic pace that is apparently independent of the emergence of other cognitive systems (e.g., Hamburger and Crain 1984). There is also a growing body of data demonstrating the emergence of linguistic principles that are not attested in the environment (e.g., Crain and Nakayama 1987; Crain and McKee 1985; Crain, Thornton, and Murasugi 1987). These findings sustain the notion that the language apparatus is a biologically coherent system, as the modularity hypothesis maintains.

A somewhat different notion of autonomy has been invoked in discussions of language processing (for example, see Fodor 1983). Here, the essential tenet concerns the locus of interaction of cognitive systems. Language processing is modular, according to this viewpoint, because, while in the process of receiving input, it is sealed off from other systems, so that a person's beliefs, desires, etc., do not exert their influence during language processing per se, but only after the autonomous grammatical processor has completed its work. In Fodor's terms, the language processor is "informationally encapsulated."

One source of evidence of the autonomy of grammar in this sense is the fact that peculiar, revolutionary, and false sentences are readily understood. To my knowledge, the argument was given first by Forster (1979). The point of the argument can be seen using sentences as simple as 1:

1. Mice chase cats.

Suppose we were to try to assign a meaning to the words in 1 without attention to syntax, say by trying to combine their meanings in a way that appears to make sense. If so, we would misunderstand it, taking it to mean that cats chase mice. The essential role of syntax in sentence processing, Forster concludes, is supported by the finding that we correctly understand sentences like this despite their a priori implausibility. To take another simple example: however unlikely it is that doctors are cured by patients, we can understand sentences such as 2, should the occasion arise in which they are true.

2. The doctor was cured by the patient.

So the function of syntax on the modularity perspective is that it allows us to describe the world no matter how unexpected things turn out to be. To underscore the point, Forster adds that the most advantageous way to construct a human brain would be to insulate syntax as much as possible from the influences of inference and beliefs about the real world. Evidence of the primacy of syntax over pragmatics by two- to four-year-old children is presented by S. Crain (1986) and Crain and McKee (1985).

An extension of the modularity hypothesis would have the language faculty itself divided into autonomous subcomponents: the lexicon, the phonology, the syntax, and the semantics. In addition, there are the processors that serve them: working memory, the syntactic parser, and so on. Several proposals have been advanced concerning the interaction of these component systems of the language apparatus during sentence processing. An early proposal, again by Forster, was that language processing is composed of discrete stages organized in a hierarchical, bottom-up fashion such that semantic processing, for instance, is not begun until lexical look-up and syntactic analysis have been completed. A less restrictive position has been advanced by Crain and Steedman (1985), who maintain the hierarchical and directional character of linguistic subcomponents, but make a different claim about their time course. On this model, the syntactic component yields as many separate structural analyses as are consistent with the input; the semantic component selects from among these. In other words, syntax proposes and semantics disposes of structural analyses *on-line*.

Following the guidelines of the extended modularity perspective, the next section contains an overview of the processing mechanisms in which language breakdown may be incurred. Then, some procedures are considered that have been employed in constructing tests to distinguish the various structures and processors involved in language performance—a development that is crucial if we are to find out what linguistic knowledge is spared and what is lost in populations that fail to exhibit normal language behavior. As noted, the research tools I will describe were developed to study language acquisition and will be applied in this paper to the problem of reading disability. But it is worth noting that these tools have also proven useful in the study of aphasia and mental retardation (W. M. Crain 1986; Shankweiler, Crain, Gorrell and Tuller, forthcoming). The common thread in this research is the finding that limitations in processing sometimes masquerade as structural deficits. To see this more clearly, the next section presents an overview of the architecture of the language understanding system.

The Language Processing System: An Overview

As a first cut at stating what is involved in sentence understanding, it will be useful to survey briefly the various tasks that are performed. For simplicity, the survey is limited to levels above phonological and morphological analysis and to the role these higher components play in conventional measures of sentence understanding such as object manipulation. The partial list is given in 3.

3. *a*) syntactic parsing
   b) semantic composition
   c) planning
   d) pragmatic presuppositions
   e) working memory

Syntactic Parsing

To begin the survey, one of the tasks in sentence understanding is to parse the test sentences (roughly, to assign to them a syntactic structure). Parsing is a dynamic process that is known to abide by certain scheduling and selection routines in accessing linguistic rules and resolving ambiguities that arise. For instance, a powerful general tendency in sentence parsing is to attach an incoming word as low in the phrase marker as possible. This is what Kimball (1973) called *Right Association* and what Frazier and Fodor (1978) call *Late Closure*. We refer to it here as Right Association. Consider this example: Suppose a boy is looking through a keyhole at a dog jumping through a hoop. How would you answer 4 in this situation?

4. What is the boy watching the dog jump through?

There are two correct answers, either "the hoop" or "the keyhole." Which answer is given depends on whether the preposition *through* is attached low in the phrase marker, as a modifier of the verb *jump,* or high, as modifying the verb *watching.* The parsing strategy of Right Association predicts that English speakers will favor the structural interpretation of the question that evokes the answer "the hoop" since this interpretation results from low attachment of the preposition *through.* Right Association also predicts that a semantically implausible reading of 5 will be pursued, at least initially. If so, 5 will be taken to mean that the dog jumped through the eye of the needle, not that the boy was watching the dog through it.

5. The boy is watching the dog jump through the eye of a needle.
Compare: He was watching him sleep through his new binoculars.

It has been argued that working memory limitations are the source of the kind of on-line integration that Right Association promotes (Frazier and Fodor 1978). This argument leads us to expect that populations with greater than normal limitations in memory will be even more dependent on parsing strategies (Shankweiler and Crain 1986). Positive results on this question were obtained in a study of preschool children by Crain and Fodor (1985).

Semantic Composition

Continuing our investigation of performance factors that are tapped in comprehension tasks, another component is semantic interpretation. Here much less is known, but it is self evident that even if a subject successfully parses an experimental sentence, he must assign a semantic representation to it. This representation is based on the lexical semantic properties of the string, which are combined according to compositional rules for deriving higher-level representations from lower-level units of meaning. Just as in syntax, process-related preferences might exist among semantic structures. And if the semantic preferences do not mirror the syntactic ones, potentially costly structural revisions might be needed in going from syntactic to semantic structure.

Planning

Once syntactic and semantic representations have been composed, the subject must plan a sequence of actions to convince his interlocutor that he does indeed understand the sentence. Samples of the syntax, semantics and plan corresponding to the phrase "the third ball" appear in figures 1 through 3.

A plan is a mental representation used to guide action. A plan may be simple in structure, consisting of just a list of statements (e.g., tests) to be performed in sequence, or it can be internally complex, with loops and branches. As figure 3 illustrates, a plan may include other cognitive steps such as evaluation conditions that determine what action to perform next, as in the "exit tests" in lines 7 and 10. Line 7 permits the exit from the inner loop only if the current sensory-attention item in the display is a ball, in which case the current mental-attention-item, an integer, is incremented. The outer loop is exited (line 10) when mental-attention-item-#1 is the same as mental-attention-item-#2 (line 3), namely the number 3. This happens when the inner loop has been circled three times, i.e., when the third ball is encountered.[1]

A cursory comparison of these candidate structures shows the plan corresponding to "third ball" to be quite complex. It is more complex, it seems, than either its syntactic or semantic

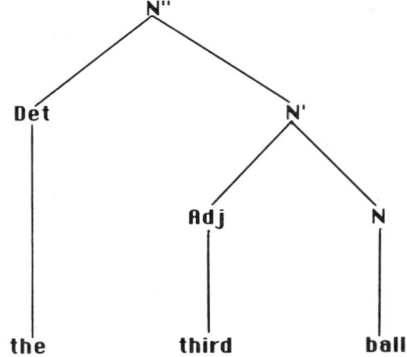

Fig. 1 Syntax of "the third ball"

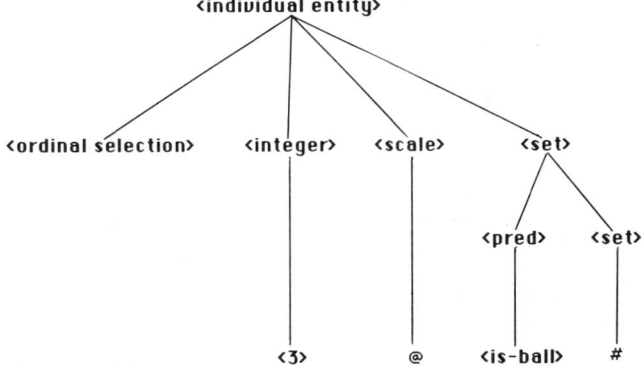

Fig. 2. Semantics of "the third ball"

structure. We are led to this conclusion by the finding that children who can deal with the individual words that make up phrases with ordinals and other types of adjectives, nevertheless fail to interpret the phrases themselves correctly except in contexts where planning characteristics are simplified.[2]

An example will be helpful in illustrating the importance of plans. Consider the observation made by Matthei (1982) and Roeper (1972) that four to six year olds have difficulty in inter-

```
1  sensory-attention-item <-- initialize (display, left-right)
2  mental-attention-item-#1 <-- initialize (numbers, low-high)
3  mental-attention-item-#2 <-- 3
4  loop
5     loop
6        sensory-attention-item <-- next (display, left-right)
7        exit-test: is-ball (sensory-attention-item)
8     endloop
9     mental-attention-item-#1 <-- next (numbers, low-high)
10    exit-test: mental-attention-item-#1 = mental-attention-item-#2
11 endloop
12 return (sensory-attention-item)
```

Fig. 3. Plan for "the third ball"

preting phrases such as *the second striped ball*. When children were confronted with arrays such as in figure 4, they often selected item *ii*, that is, the ball that is second in the array and also is striped, rather than item *iv*, which is the second of the striped balls (counting from the left).

The empirical finding, then, is that children assign an interpretation that is not the same as an adult would assign to expressions of this kind. This difference is attributed by Matthei to children's failure to adopt the hierarchical phrase structure of noun phrases that characterizes the adult grammar. Instead, he argues that they adopt a "flat structure" for phrases of this kind.

It is clear the "flat structure" analysis depends on the premise that a child's semantic interpretation directly reflects the syntactic structure being assigned to a string, i.e., that syntactic and semantic analyses are isomorphic, rather than autonomous. Since the syntax and semantics of these phrases are not isomor-

Why Poor Readers Misunderstand Spoken Sentences 147

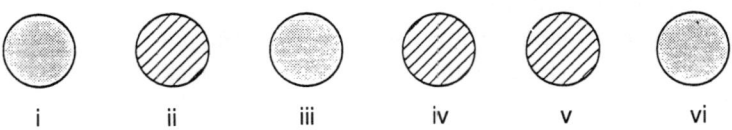

Fig. 4. Array for "the second striped ball"

phic in the adult grammar, this means that children would be hypothesizing a nonadult grammar.

Any divergence that may exist between children's and adults' grammars poses a problem from the standpoint of language acquisition; namely, explaining how children ultimately converge on the adult grammar. In the present case, the problem of *transition* from the infant's initial state to mastery of the adult grammar has received critical attention in the linguistic literature. Hornstein and Lightfoot (1981) argue that if children adopted nonadult phrase structure rules that generate trees such as 6, rather than an adult tree such as 7, evidence would not be available in the environment to purge their grammars of the incorrect analysis. The evidence that would justify the abandonment of the illicit analysis could, in principle, be supplied by corrective feedback, but it is widely held that this kind of data is not systematically available to children. If Hornstein and Lightfoot are correct, then, any explanation of children's errors invoking a "flat" phrase marker runs headlong into the problem of "unlearning."

6.   7.

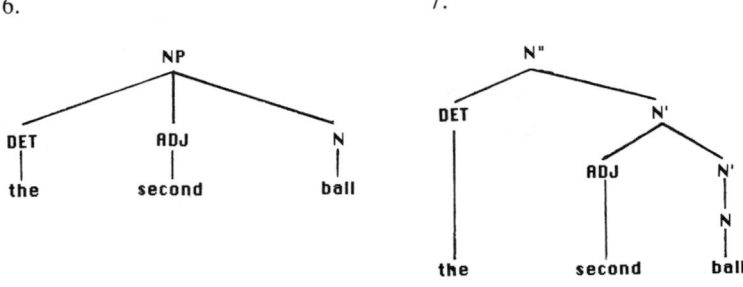

To avoid this problem, Hornstein and Lightfoot propose, as an innate principle of Universal Grammar (in particular, X-bar theory), that children initially hypothesize rules that establish intermediate level syntactic constituents like N'. They contend that the rules generating 6 could never be entertained as part of children's early grammars. In short, they would explicitly deny the "flat structure" explanation of children's errors, which is based on the assumption that children initially adopt rules that generate trees without intermediate level categories.

Fortunately, there is an alternative component of the language processor in which the errors might have arisen. As with the phrase *third ball*, the logical structure of the necessary plan for *second striped ball* is quite complex. This suggests that *plan* complexity, and not syntactic complexity, could be the source of children's errors in locating the designated object.

An explanation of children's errors in terms of the foregoing analysis of plan complexity has received empirical support. A dramatic improvement in children's responses to the target phrases resulted from two changes in method, implemented in successive experiments by Hamburger and Crain (1984). One change was the inclusion of a pretask session in which the children handled and counted homogeneous subsets of the items that were subsequently used in the test arrays. This experience served to prime in advance some of the planning required in the main experimental task. Further improvement in performance on phrases like *second striped ball* resulted from first asking the child to identify the *first* striped ball, thus forcing the child to plan and execute part of the plan used in interpreting the target phrase. Facilitating the planning aspects of the task by these stepwise, simplifying maneuvers thus made it possible for children to reveal mastery of the syntax and semantics of such expressions.

A positive result from the standpoint of language learnability was also obtained in the Hamburger and Crain study. On the Hornstein and Lightfoot account, the proform "one" is coreferential with the intermediate level constituent N' and not the lexical level constituent N. They predict that as soon as children understand the meaning of ordinals they should permit "one" to corefer with "green ball" in response to situations like the one depicted in 8; that is, they should sometimes point to *v*.

8. Instructions: Point to the first green ball; point to the second *one*.

GREEN SQUARE	RED SQUARE	GREEN BALL	RED BALL	GREEN BALL	RED BALL
i	*ii*	*iii*	*iv*	*v*	*vi*

This is precisely what was found by Hamburger and Crain. In fact, children consistently used the proform "one" to corefer with expressions like "green ball." Notice that using "one" in this way is incompatible with the "flat structure" account, given the standard assumption in linguistics that proforms corefer with a syntactic constituent. Since "green ball" does not form a constituent on this account, children should only have been able to interpret "the second one" to mean the second *ball iv*, not the second *green ball v*.

The findings in these experiments undermine the "flat structure" account of children's nonadult interpretations and provide empirical support for the early mastery of one aspect of Universal Grammar that has been motivated on theoretical grounds by consideration of the logical problem of language learnability in the absence of negative data. Most important for our purposes, the findings underscore the contributions of planning in language processing. They defy explanation on the view that a lack of syntactic knowledge was responsible for children's errors in the earlier studies on prenominal modifiers. For several other constructions it has been possible to design experiments that minimize the impact of the extraneous factors of planning and parsing while investigating children's knowledge of linguistic structure. With appropriate attention paid to process it is found that children produce and understand syntactic structures of considerable complexity. Their performance failures, previously imputed to lack of syntactic knowledge, receive a better accounting in terms of the relative complexity of processing factors associated with the test sentences.

Presupposition

The formation of a cognitive plan is not the only factor that has been found to mask knowledge of syntactic principles. Test sentences whose pragmatic presuppositions are unsatisfied in the experimental situation have been found to result in inaccurate assessments of structural knowledge—for both normal and reading disabled children, and for mentally retarded adults. Let us consider an experiment that points out the relevance of presuppositional content in sentence understanding.

This experiment used the contrast between two structural phenomena, coordination and subordination. It is widely held that structures that involve subordination are more complex than ones involving coordination. Researchers in language acquisition have appealed to this difference to explain why children typically make more errors in understanding sentences bearing relative clauses (as in 9) than sentences containing conjoined clauses (as in 10), when comprehension is assessed by a figure manipulation ("do-what-I-say") task.

9. The dog pushed the sheep that jumped over the fence.
10. The dog pushed the sheep and jumped over the fence.

The usual finding that 9 is more difficult for children than 10 has been interpreted as evidence for the relatively late emergence of the rules for subordinate syntax in language development (e.g., Tavakolian 1981). However, it was shown by Hamburger and Crain (1982) that the source of children's performance errors on this task was *not* a lack of syntactic knowledge. By constructing pragmatic contexts in which the presuppositions of restrictive relative clauses were satisfied, they were able to demonstrate mastery of relative clause structure by children as young as three. There are two presuppositions in 9: (*i*) that there are at least two sheep in the context and (*ii*) that one of the sheep jumped over a fence prior to the utterance. Young children reliably produce meaningful utterances with relative clauses when these "felicity conditions" are met. This is strong presumptive evidence that absence of context or infelicitous contexts in previous studies masked children's competence with this construction.

Working Memory

To complete the survey, we turn to the role of working memory in language processing. A point of terminology must be noted: "short-term memory" is not the same as "working memory," although the former is partly subsumed by the latter. Short-term memory is commonly viewed as a passive storage bin for information, whereas working memory is a dynamic processing system, although it has a storage component. (There is now widespread agreement on this point, e.g., Baddeley and Hitch 1974; Daneman and Carpenter 1980; Perfetti and Lesgold 1979; Shankweiler and Crain 1986.) Our concern is with working memory, and primarily with its operational aspect.

On the simplest analysis, verbal working memory has just two parts. One is a storage buffer, where rehearsal of phonetically coded material takes place. Without continuous rehearsal, unorganized linguistic information (for example, a telephone number) can be stored only briefly, perhaps for only a second or two without rehearsal. Let us refer to this as the *aggregation problem*. To solve this problem, the language processing mechanism must rapidly analyze incoming material into units corresponding to its levels of structural representation, i.e., the phonology, the lexicon, the syntax, and the semantics. This solution was aptly referred to by Miller (1956) as *chunking* in his investigations of the capacity of immediate memory.

After material in the short-term storage buffer receives its initial, phonological representation, it is shunted to the next level of representation. This is accomplished by the second component of working memory, the "executive" component. Pursuing an analogy with the compiling of programming languages, it can be viewed as a *control structure* that fits together "statements" from the phonological, syntactic, and semantic parsers. On this conception, the control structure facilitates the integration of the products of lower-level processing at higher levels by relaying information that has undergone analysis upward through the system, thereby freeing the buffer for new phonological input. In both reading and speech, working memory serves to regulate the flow of linguistic material from lower to higher levels of representation. In the following sections, we consider how abnormal limitations of working memory might interfere with sentence understanding both by eye and by ear. Our first topic is comprehension of spoken sentences by young children.

A potential impediment to successful comprehension involves the presuppositions of the sentences used to test competence (see Hamburger and Crain 1982, 1984). Recall that when presuppositions were satisfied in an act-out task with children, their comprehension improved dramatically.[3] I would suggest that working memory is stressed when presuppositions go unmet. It should be noted in this connection that even children's *correct* responses to sentences containing relative clauses can be seen to display the effects of memory demands on sentence comprehension. Thus, Hamburger and Crain (1982) found that many children who performed the correct actions associated with sentences such as 11 often failed, nevertheless, to act out these events in the same way as adults.

11. The dog pushed the sheep that jumped over the fence.

Most three year olds and many four year olds acted out this sentence by making the dog push the sheep first, and then making the sheep jump over the fence. Older children and normal adults act out these events in the opposite order, the relative clause *before* the main clause. Intuitively, acting out the second mentioned clause first seems conceptually more correct since "the sheep that jumped over the fence" is what the dog pushed.

It is reasonable to suppose that this kind of conflict between the order of mention and conceptual order stresses working memory because both clauses must be available long enough to enable the hearer to plan the response which represents the conceptual order. Let us call this the *sequencing problem.* Presumably, the difference in children and adults reflects the more severe limitations in children's working memory in coping with the sequencing problem. Young children are unable to hold information long enough in working memory to compile a conceptually correct plan, and so they interpret and act out clauses in an order-of-mention fashion.

Another line of research has yielded support for the twofold claim that processing factors mask children's knowledge of complex structures and that working memory is specifically implicated. Temporal terms like *before, after,* and *while* dictate the conceptual order of events, and they too may present sequencing problems, that is, conflicts between conceptual order and order of mention. This is illustrated in sentence 12.

12. Luke flew the plane after Han flew the helicopter.

In this example, a sequencing problem arises because the order in which events are mentioned is opposite the conceptual order. Again, research in language acquisition has found that young children frequently interpret these sentences in an order-of-mention fashion (Clark 1970; Johnson 1975). As with relative clause sentences, it is likely that this response reflects an inability to hold both clauses in memory long enough to formulate a plan for acting them out in the correct conceptual order.

There is direct evidence that the sequencing problem created by the requirements of plan formation, and not lack of syntactic or semantic competence, is responsible for children's errors in comprehending sentences with temporal terms (Crain 1982; Gorrell, Crain, and Fodor 1986; Macaruso et al., forthcoming).

The evidence is this: once working memory demands are reduced, most four- and five-year-old children usually give the correct response to sentences such as 13.

13. Push the plane to me after you push the helicopter.

To minimize memory load, the procedure, once again, was to take cognizance of the presuppositions on the use of temporal terms. The presupposition associated with sentence 13 is that the hearer intends to push a helicopter. To satisfy this presupposition, one simply has to ask the subject *in advance* to select one of the toys to play with before each trial. When children were given this contextual support they displayed unprecedented success in comprehending the temporal terms *before* and *after*. In a recent study with mentally retarded adults, it was found that they too displayed unprecedented success in understanding sentences with temporal terms when presuppositions were met (W. M. Crain 1986). The performance level went from 54 percent correct without contextual support to 81 percent correct in more felicitous contexts. A control group of mentally retarded adults, who simply performed the task twice, showed no improvement whatsoever. Findings such as these underscore the special need to control for pragmatic factors when our goal is to identify the source of performance failures in a language impaired population. What looked like a deficiency in syntactic competence turned out, on closer inspection, to be failure in processing caused by a less than optimal context, that is, a context that failed to satisfy presuppositions.

Applied Modularity: A Case Study

Three steps would appear to be jointly sufficient to tease apart a structural deficit from a limitation in processing. The first step is to establish, perhaps by means of a pretest, that the subjects in our experiments have the necessary prerequisites for successful comprehension of the target sentences. If we fail to make this check we may easily mistake a deficit at the level of the word for a deficit at the sentence level; a subject who does not understand the meaning of the individual words that make up a phrase or sentence can hardly be expected to reveal knowledge of its syntactic or semantic structure.

In the second step in the diagnosis, the structural properties of sentences are held constant while processing load is varied. The variables one chooses to manipulate will depend on which processing component is assumed to be responsible. For example, if errors are seen as a consequence of limited working memory capacity, then either the semantic content of the stimulus sentences can be altered, or the sentences can be embedded in contexts that impose minimal demands on working memory. If performance failures in ordinary circumstances reflect a processing limitation, then the subjects' performance should show appreciable improvement when processing load is reduced. It seems clear that if a structural deficit is responsible for subjects' poor performance, simply minimizing processing demands should result in no appreciable increase in correct responding.

The third critical step in distinguishing structural versus processing explanations of performance errors is to examine the data for evidence of *competence* with the structure under investigation. Competence can be inferred if subjects' performance sufficiently approaches 100 percent correct responses under optimal conditions. To my knowledge, the search for "optimal performability" was first articulated in the research literature on aphasia by Caramazza and Zurif (1976).

Another place to look for evidence of a processing deficit is in the pattern of errors. Here the distinction between a limitation in processing and a structural deficit may be revealed by comparing the pattern of responses of subjects from the target population with those of an appropriate control group (see Shankweiler, Crain, Brady, and Macaruso, forthcoming). A processing account could explain cases in which both the experimental group and the control group maintain the same proportion of errors across sentence types. In other words, the experimental group should show a comparable decrement in performance for each sentence type (or for each subtype of linguistic construction). Statistically speaking, processing limitations predict a main effect of group on the test sentences, but no interaction of group by sentence type. By contrast, a structural deficit would usually predict an interaction of group by sentence type, with performance on at least one sentence type at chance (or below) for the language impaired population. The question of a structural versus a processing account of performance failures presses for an answer in many arenas. The remainder of the paper will show how these principles for analysis of a language deficit can be applied to the problem of understanding reading disability. Further examples may be found in the chapter by Shankweiler in this volume.

It has been mentioned that children with reading disorders frequently exhibit poor performance on many measures of language skills, including comprehension of spoken sentences with complex syntactic structures, e.g., relative clauses and adjectives of object control such as *easy,* which were contrasted with subject control adjectives such as *eager.* It is claimed by Byrne (1981) that children with reading difficulties tend to treat adjectives like *easy* as if they are subject control adjectives like *eager.* This proposal is based, for the most part, on an experiment on poor readers, but in the background is Carol Chomsky's (1969) finding that normal children as old as nine or ten sometimes interpret the subject of sentences such as 14 as the subject of the infinitival clause. That is, they were interpreting 14 as if it meant "The bear can reach (the honey) easily." By contrast, such a subject control interpretation is correct for 15.

14. The bear is easy to reach.
15. The bear is eager to reach.

Such findings have led several researchers including Byrne to suggest that the comprehension failures of reading disabled children stem from a developmental lag in acquisition of complex syntactic structures (see also Stein, Cairns, and Zurif 1984; Vogel 1975).

Elsewhere we have reviewed studies that have found poor readers inferior on some measure of comprehension of spoken sentences (Shankweiler and Crain 1986; Shankweiler, in this volume). In each case, it was shown that the research failed to conform completely to the formula given above for assessing grammatical competence. For example, the subjects in Byrne's study were not pretested for knowledge of the meanings of the adjectives that appeared in the stimulus sentences, and no attempt was made to hold processing demands to a minimum. It is also pertinent to note that most previous work failed to attend to the "felicity conditions" for the use of an adjective such as *easy*. Sentence 14 was presented in situations in which the relative ease of reaching the bear was not established in advance.

These methodological considerations call into question the conclusion that reading disability reflects a syntactic deficit and raise the possibility that poor readers suffer instead from a limitation in information processing, perhaps a limitation in working memory. When Byrne visited us recently, we decided to pit the syntactic deficit account of poor readers' sentence comprehension difficulties against a processing explanation.

In this collaborative study, children's knowledge of adjectives of object control such as *easy* was assessed in three separate tests. Each test used a forced choice task with pairs of pictures: First, there was a test of the critical lexical items in their simplest use. For this test, sentences such as 16 were presented.

16. It is easy to reach the bear.

As figure 5 shows, in one picture a very large bear is reaching for honey; in the other, a boy is reaching for a bear that is readily accessible because the cage door is open. If failures had occurred in response to a sentence such as 16, it would have been pointless to proceed with any of the further tests. How-

Fig. 5. Alternative pictures for "The bear is easy to reach"

ever, this test was administered last in order to eliminate any response bias that may obtain from encountering the target adjectives in this simple format.

A test of the harder case was also included, namely *The bear is easy to reach,* using the same pairs of pictures used for 16. This test explicitly contrasted a depiction of the *incorrect* subject control interpretation with the *correct* object control interpretation. A child with the incorrect grammatical analysis should consistently pick the wrong picture. Again, the pictures satisfied the felicity conditions for the adjective.

In this study another step was taken to verify that the processing component assumed to be the source of the performance failures is actually the responsible factor. This search for preferences among syntactic structures was undertaken on the assumption that the syntactic parser was the source of performance failures in previous research. To verify this, we asked subjects to respond to ambiguous sentences in order to examine their parsing preferences. Ambiguous sentences were included, such as 17, with pictures corresponding to both readings of the sentence, as figure 6 illustrates.

17. The man is too dirty to serve.

Focusing on this figure, notice that in one picture a dirty man is not being allowed to serve a disgusted woman; in the other picture a dirty man is being refused service. Sentence 17 is a correct description of either picture. A test of responses to ambiguous sentences was included in this study to discover whether the unconscious adoption of a parsing strategy was encouraging the poor readers to assign subject control in cases where both control possibilities exist in the adult grammar. If so, they would be expected to favor the picture in which the filthy man is serving the food to the woman.[4]

The subjects were forty-four good and forty-six poor readers in the second grade. We found that, for three of the four adjectives, both groups performed nearly without error in identifying the picture that corresponded with the correct, object control interpretation. In striking contrast to previous research, even the poor reader group gave over 90 percent correct responses when task demands were controlled.[5] With the ambiguous sentences, it was found that responses indicating an object control interpretation were nearly as frequent as subject con-

Fig. 6. Alternative pictures for "The man is too dirty to serve"

trol responses for both groups, and again there was no difference between groups (good readers = 51 percent; poor readers = 55 percent). This means that the errors by poor readers in previous studies cannot be explained as the reflection of a parsing preference for subject control. So we were wrong in our speculation about the source of their errors. An explanation will have to be sought elsewhere. Finally, both reader groups responded correctly more than 90 percent of the time to simplified sentences such as 16. Once again there were no group differences.

The conclusion to draw from these results is that in earlier work the grammatical competence of poor readers was masked by performance factors. When questions about syntactic knowledge were asked in a different way, by adopting a task that reduces as far as possible the *nonsyntactic* demands in a comprehension test, children diagnosed as cases of specific reading disability were found to succeed. Although the possibility must be left open that some linguistic structures are problematic for children reaching the age at which reading instruction normally begins, this line of research emphasizes how much syntax has already been mastered by these children (Crain and Shankweiler 1988). The failure in previous work to control for nonsyntactic contributions to the total task of sentence comprehension has surely led to underestimates of the grammatical capabilities of poor readers.

Conclusion

This chapter outlined two prerequisites to the construction of a bridge between linguistic theory and research on reading disability. The first is an explicit characterization of the processing mechanisms in which linguistic representations are couched. The second prerequisite is in the area of experimental methodology, where we have seen that theoretical proposals depend on successful efforts to disentangle the subcomponents of the language apparatus that are intertwined in ordinary language use. In this area, theoretical insights await technological innovations, but there have been some successes in identifying the source of performance failures in children with reading disorder. We have seen how the apparent failure of poor readers on a linguistic structure can result from the influence of nonsyntactic factors that mask their knowledge of syntax. New techniques have resulted in demonstrations of mastery of complex syntax in young children and older children with reading disability. We are beginning to discover that this also holds true of other language impaired populations. In closing, I wish to underscore that the bridge between linguistic theory and experimental research ought to be made to bear two-way traffic. On one side, linguistic theory and theories of sentence processing enable us to advance specific proposals about language acquisition and reading; on the other, the findings from appropriate experimental studies can help us see which theoretical proposals are closer to the truth.

NOTES

Parts of this research were supported by NSF Grant BNS 84-18537 and by a Program Project Grant to Haskins Laboratories from the National Institute of Child Health and Human Development (HD-01994). This chapter is adapted from Crain, "On performability: Structure and process in language understanding," *Clinical Linguistics and Phonetics 1* (1987): 127–45. I am indebted to Donald Shankweiler and Henry Hamburger for discussion of the issues in this chapter.

1. Some comments about figures 1 and 2 are also in order. The syntactic structure in figure 1 uses X-bar notation (Jackendoff 1977). This representation says that a noun phrase (N″) consists of a determiner (Det) and an intermediate level category (N′) which itself is made up of an adjective and a noun.

The semantic structure in figure 2, adapted from Hamburger and Crain (1987), begins with a root node labeled <individual entity> because the referent of the phrase will be an individual, as opposed to a set. The terminal node # stands for a set of entities to be provided by a real-world situation. The predicate <is-ball> determines a subset of those entities at the next level up. The ordinal third (<3>) also requires a scale @, e.g., left-to-right ordering.

2. It is worth noting that even if an appropriate plan has been compiled, the subject must ultimately deal with real-world objects in order to demonstrate understanding. The execution of plans introduces yet another layer of complexity, depending on the specifics of the task. The plan might be realized as an utterance, as an ordered sequence of actions, as selection of an object from an array, and so on.

3. The reason is that when presuppositions are flouted, the listener has extra computations to perform. Namely, the listener must "increment" his or her mental model of the discourse to bring it in line with the presuppositions that were implied by the speaker. This process is explained more fully in Crain and Steedman (1985).

4. Each subject responded to eight sentences patterned like 14, and to four examples of each of the other types. Four adjectives were used (easy, hard, difficult, and impossible), always followed by the same verb (reach, catch, chase, and jump, respectively).

5. It should be noted, however, that many children in each group chose the incorrect picture for sentences such as *i*, presumably because *jump* can only be used intransitively in some dialects.

i) The frog is impossible to jump.

REFERENCES

Baddeley, A. D., and Hitch, G. B. 1974. Working memory. In *The Psychology of Learning and Motivation*, vol. 8, ed. G. H. Bower. New York: Academic Press.

Byrne, B. 1981. Deficient syntactic control in poor readers: Is a weak phonetic memory code responsible? *Applied Psycholinguistics* 2: 210–12.

Caramazza, A., and Zurif, E. B. 1976. Dissociation of algorithmic and heuristic processes in language comprehension: Evidence from aphasia. *Brain and Language* 3:572–82.

Chomsky, C. 1970. *On Language and Learning from 5 to 10: The Acquisition of Syntax in Children.* Cambridge, Mass.: MIT Press.

Clark, E. V. 1970. How young children describe events in time. In *Advances in Psycholinguistics,* ed. G. B. Flores d'Arcais and W. J. M. Levelt. Amsterdam: North Holland.

Crain, S. 1982. Temporal terms: Mastery by age five. *Papers and Reports on Child Language Development,* vol. 21. Stanford: Stanford University.

———. 1986. On the developmental autonomy of syntax. Paper presented at the Eleventh Annual Boston University Conference on Child Language Development, Boston, Mass.

Crain, S., and Fodor, J. 1985. On the innateness of Subjacency. *Proceedings of the Eastern States Conference on Linguistics,* vol. 1. Columbus: Ohio State University.

Crain, S., and McKee, C. 1985. Acquisition of structural constraints on anaphora. Proceedings of the *Northeastern Linguistic Society* 16. Amherst, Mass.: University of Massachusetts.

Crain, S., and Nakayama, M. 1987. Structure-dependence in grammar formation. *Language* 63:522–43.
Crain, S., and Shankweiler, D. 1988. Syntactic complexity and reading acquisition. In *Linguistic Complexity and Text Comprehension: Readability Issues Reconsidered,* ed. A. Davison and G. M. Green. Hillsdale, N.J.: Erlbaum.
Crain, S., and Steedman M. 1985. On not being led up the garden path: The use of context by the syntactic processor. In *Natural Language Parsing: Psychological, Computational, and Theoretical Perspectives,* ed. D. R. Dowty, L. Karttunen, and A. Zwicky. Cambridge: Cambridge University Press.
Crain, S.; Thornton, R.; and Murasugi, K. 1987. Capturing the evasive passive. Paper presented at the Twelfth Annual Boston University Conference on Language Development, Boston, Mass.
Crain, W. M. 1986. Restrictions on the comprehension of syntax by mentally retarded adults. Ph.D. diss., Claremont Graduate School, Claremont, Calif.
Daneman, M., and Carpenter, P. A. 1980. Individual differences in working memory and reading. *Journal of Verbal Learning and Verbal Behavior* 19:450–66.
Fodor, J. A. 1983. *The Modularity of Mind.* Cambridge, Mass.: MIT Press.
Forster, K. 1979. Levels of processing and the structure of the language processor. In *Sentence Processing: Studies Presented to Merrill Garrett,* ed. W. E. Cooper and E. C. T. Walker. Hillsdale, N.J.: Erlbaum.
Frazier, L., and Fodor, J. D. 1978. The sausage machine: A new two-stage parsing model. *Cognition* 6:291–325.
Gorrell, P.; Crain, S.; and Fodor, J. D. 1986. Contextual information and temporal terms. Paper presented at the Eleventh Annual Boston University Conference on Language Development, Boston, Mass.
Hamburger, H., and Crain, S. 1982. Relative acquisition. In *Language Development.* vol. 1, *Syntax and Semantics,* ed. S. Kucjaz II. Hillsdale, N.J.: Erlbaum.
———. 1984. Acquisition of cognitive compiling. *Cognition* 17:85–136.
———. 1987. Plans and semantics in human processing of language. *Cognitive Science* 11:101–36.
Hornstein, N., and Lightfoot, D. 1981. Introduction to *Explanation in Linguistics: The Logical Problem of Language Acquisition,* ed. N. Hornstein and D. Lightfoot. New York: Longman.
Jackendoff, R. 1977. *X-bar Syntax: A Study of Phrase Structure.* Cambridge, Mass.: MIT Press.

Johnson, M. L. 1975. The meaning of *before* and *after* for preschool children. *Journal of Experimental Child Psychology* 19:88–99.

Kimball, J. 1973. Seven principles of surface structure parsing in natural language. *Cognition* 2:15–47.

Liberman, A., and Mattingly, I. G. 1985. The motor theory of speech perception revisited. *Cognition* 21:1–36.

Macaruso, P.; Bar-Shalom, E.; Crain, S.; and Shankweiler, D. Forthcoming. Comprehension of temporal terms by good and poor readers. *Language and Speech* 32.

Matthei, E. M. 1982. The acquisition of prenominal modifier sequences. *Cognition* 11:301–32.

Miller, G. A. 1956. The magic number seven plus or minus two, or, some limits on our capacity for processing information. *Psychological Review* 63:81–96.

Perfetti, C. A., and Lesgold, A. M. 1979. Coding and comprehension in skilled reading and implications for reading instruction. In *Theory and Practice of Early Reading*, ed. L. B. Resnick and P. Weaver. Hillsdale, N.J.: Erlbaum.

Roeper, T. 1972. Approaches to a theory of language acquisition with examples from German children. Ph.D. diss., Harvard University.

Shankweiler, D., and Crain, S. 1986. Language mechanisms and reading disorder: A modular approach. *Cognition* 24:139–68.

Shankweiler, D.; Crain, S.; Brady, S.; and Macaruso, P. Forthcoming. Identifying the causes of reading disability. In *Reading Acquisition*, ed. P. B. Gough. Hillsdale, N.J.: Erlbaum.

Shankweiler, D.; Crain, S.; Gorrell, P.; and Tuller, B. Forthcoming. Reception of language in agrammatism: Evidence of preserved syntactic competence. *Language and Cognitive Processes*.

Stein, C. L.; Cairns, H. S.; and Zurif, E. B. 1984. Sentence comprehension limitations related to syntactic deficits in reading-disabled children. *Applied Psycholinguistics* 5:305–22.

Tavakolian, S. L. 1981. The conjoined-clause analysis of relative clauses. In *Language Acquisition and Linguistic Theory*, ed. S. Tavakolian. Cambridge, Mass.: MIT Press.

Vogel, S. A. 1975. *Syntactic Abilities in Normal and Dyslexic Children*. Baltimore, Md.: University Park Press.

Whitaker, H. 1976. A case of the isolation of the language function. In *Studies in Neurolinguistics*, vol. 2, ed. H. Whitaker and H. A. Whitaker. New York: Academic Press.

Contributors

Each of the authors, with the exception of William E. Tunmer, is a research associate of Haskins Laboratories, 270 Crown Street, New Haven, CT 06511. The authors' names and the other institutions with which they are affiliated are listed below:

Stephen Crain, Ph.D., Department of Linguistics, U-145, University of Connecticut, Storrs, CT 06269.

Vicki L. Hanson, Ph.D., IBM Research Division, Thomas J. Watson Research Center, P. O. Box 218, Yorktown Heights, NY 10598.

Alvin M. Liberman, Ph.D., Emeritus, Department of Psychology, University of Connecticut, Storrs, CT 06269, and Emeritus, Department of Linguistics, Yale University, New Haven, CT 06520.

Isabelle Y. Liberman, Ph.D., FIARLD, Emerita, Department of Educational Psychology, University of Connecticut, Storrs, CT 06269.

Donald Shankweiler, Ph.D., FIARLD, Department of Psychology, U-20, University of Connecticut, Storrs, CT 06269.

William E. Tunmer, Ph.D., Department of Education, Massey University, Palmerston North, New Zealand.

International Academy for Research in Learning Disabilities Monograph Series

Syracuse University Press
> *A System of Marker Variables for the Field of Learning Disabilities*
> Barbara K. Keogh et al.

The University of Michigan Press
> *Rhyme and Reason in Reading and Spelling*
> Lynette Bradley and Peter Bryant
>
> *Drugs in Pregnancy and Childbirth: Infant Exposure and Maternal Information*
> Yvonne Brackbill, Karen McManus, and Lynn Woodward
>
> *Behavior Problems in Children with Developmental and Learning Disabilities*
> Robert J. Thompson, Jr.
>
> *La Normalización del Deficiente: Actitudes del Profesorado*
> (Teachers' Attitudes toward Mainstreaming Handicapped Children in Spain)
> Francisco Alberto Chueca y Mora
>
> *Neurometric Evaluation of Brain Function in Normal and Learning Disabled Children*
> E. Roy John
>
> *Phonology and Reading Disability: Solving the Reading Puzzle*
> Donald Shankweiler and Isabelle Y. Liberman, editors